THE
PERSON
& WORK
OF THE

Holy
Spirit

THE
PERSON
& WORK
OF THE

Holy Spirit

R.A. Torrey

Whitaker House

THE PERSON AND WORK OF THE HOLY SPIRIT

ISBN: 0–88368–384–9
Printed in the United States of America
Copyright © 1996 by Whitaker House

Whitaker House
580 Pittsburgh Street
Springdale, PA 15144

1 2 3 4 5 6 7 8 9 10 11 / 06 05 04 03 02 01 00 99 98 97 96

Contents

Chapter 1

The Personality of the Holy Spirit

Before one can correctly understand the work of the Holy Spirit, he must first of all know the Spirit Himself. A frequent source of error and fanaticism about the work of the Holy Spirit is the attempt to study and understand His work without first of all coming to know Him as a person.

It is of the highest importance from the standpoint of worship that we decide whether the Holy Spirit is a divine person, worthy to receive our adoration, our faith, our love, and our entire surrender to Himself, or whether it is simply an influence emanating from God or a power or an illumination that God imparts to us. If the Holy Spirit is a divine person and we do not know Him as such, then we are robbing a divine being of the worship and the faith and the love and the surrender to Himself which are His due.

It is also of the highest importance from a practical standpoint that we decide whether the Holy Spirit is merely some mysterious and wonderful power that we, in our weakness and ignorance, are somehow to get hold of and use or whether the Holy Spirit is a real person, infinitely holy, infinitely wise, infinitely mighty, and infinitely tender, who is to get hold of and use us. The former conception is utterly heathenish, not essentially different from the thought of the African fetish worshiper who has his god whom he uses. The latter conception is sublime and Christian. If we think of the Holy Spirit, as so many do, as merely a power or influence, our constant thought will be, "How can I get more of the Holy Spirit?" But if we think of Him in the biblical way as a divine person, our thought will instead be, "How can the Holy Spirit have more of me?"

The conception of the Holy Spirit as being a divine influence or power that we are somehow to get hold of and use leads to self-exaltation and self-sufficiency. One who so thinks of the Holy Spirit and who at the same time imagines that he has received the Holy Spirit will almost inevitably be full of spiritual pride and strut about as if he belonged to some superior order of Christians. One frequently hears such people say, "I am a Spirit-filled man," or "I am a Spirit-filled woman."

But if we once grasp the thought that the Holy Spirit is a divine person of infinite majesty, glory, holiness, and power, who in marvelous condescension has come into our hearts to make His abode there and take possession of our lives and make use of them, it will put us in the dust and keep us in the dust. I can think of no thought more humbling or more overwhelming than the thought that a person of divine majesty and glory dwells in my heart and is ready to use even me.

It is of the highest importance from the standpoint of experience that we know the Holy Spirit as a person. Thousands and tens of thousands of men and women can testify to the blessing that has come into their own lives as they have come to know the Holy Spirit. They have come to know the Holy Spirit not merely as a gracious influence (emanating, it is true, from God) but as a real person, just as real as Jesus Christ Himself, an ever-present, loving Friend and mighty Helper who is not only always by their sides but who dwells in their hearts every day and every hour and who is ready to undertake for them in every emergency of life. Thousands of ministers, Christian workers, and Christians in the humblest spheres of life have spoken to me or written to me of the complete transformation of their Christian experience that came to them when they grasped the thought (not merely in a theological but in an experiential way) that the Holy Spirit is a person and consequently came to know Him.

There are at least four distinct proofs in the Bible that the Holy Spirit is a person.

All the distinctive characteristics of personality are ascribed to the Holy Spirit in the Bible.

What are the distinctive characteristics, or marks, of personality? Knowledge, feeling or emotion, and will. Any entity that thinks and feels and wills is a person. When we say that the Holy Spirit is a person, there are those who understand us to mean that the Holy Spirit has hands and feet and eyes and ears and mouth and so on, but these are not the characteristics of personality but of bodily substance. All of these characteristics or marks of personality are repeatedly ascribed to the Holy Spirit in the Old and New Testaments.

We read in 1 Corinthians,

> But God hath revealed them unto us by his Spirit: for the Spirit searcheth all things, yea, the deep things of God. For what man knoweth the things of a man, save the spirit of man which is in him? even so the things of God knoweth no man, but the Spirit of God. (1 Cor. 2:10–11)

Here knowledge is ascribed to the Holy Spirit. We are clearly taught that the Holy Spirit is not merely an influence that illuminates our minds to comprehend the truth but a being who Himself knows the truth.

We also read, "But all these worketh that one and the selfsame Spirit, dividing to every man severally as he will" (1 Cor. 12:11). Here, will is ascribed to the Spirit, and we are taught that the Holy Spirit is not a power that we get hold of and use according to our desires but a person of sovereign majesty who uses us according to His will. This distinction is of fundamental importance in our getting into right relations with the Holy Spirit. It is at this very point that many honest seekers after power and efficiency in service go astray. They are reaching out after and struggling to get possession of some mysterious and mighty power that they can make use of in their work according to their own desires. They will never get possession of the power they seek until they come to recognize that there is not some divine power for them to get hold of and use in their blindness and ignorance but that there is a person, infinitely wise as well as infinitely mighty, who is willing to take possession of them and use them according to His own perfect will.

When we stop to think of it, we must rejoice that there is no divine power we beings, so ignorant and so liable to err as we are, can get hold of and use. How appalling might be the results if there were. But what a holy joy must come into our hearts when we grasp the thought that there is a divine person, One who never errs, who is willing to take possession of us and impart to us such gifts as He sees best and to use us according to His wise and loving will.

We read in Romans 8:27, "And he that searcheth the hearts knoweth what is the mind of the Spirit, because he maketh intercession for the saints according to the will of God." In this passage mind is ascribed to the Holy Spirit. The Greek word translated "mind" is a comprehensive word, including the ideas of thought, feeling, and purpose. It is the same word that is used in Romans 8:7 where we read that "the carnal mind is enmity against God: for it is not subject to the law of God, neither indeed can be." So in this verse all the distinctive marks of personality are included in the word *mind* and are ascribed to the Holy Spirit.

We find the personality of the Holy Spirit brought out in a most touching and suggestive way

11

in Romans 15:30: "Now I beseech you, brethren, for the Lord Jesus Christ's sake, and for the love of the Spirit, that ye strive together with me in your prayers to God for me." Here we have "love" ascribed to the Holy Spirit. The reader would do well to stop and ponder those five words: "the love of the Spirit."

We dwell often upon the love of God the Father. It is the subject of our daily and constant thought. We dwell often upon the love of Jesus Christ the Son. Who would think of calling himself a Christian who passed a day without meditating on the love of his Savior, but how often have we meditated upon "the love of the Spirit"?

Each day of our lives, if we are living as Christians ought, we kneel down in the presence of God the Father, look up into His face, and say, "I thank you, Father, for Your great love that led You to give Your only begotten Son to die upon the cross of Calvary for me." Each day of our lives we also look up into the face of our Lord and Savior, Jesus Christ, and say, "Oh, glorious Lord and Savior, Jesus the Son of God, I thank You for Your great love that led You not to count it a thing to be on equality with God but to empty Yourself, and forsaking all the glory of heaven, come down to earth with all its shame and to take my sins upon Yourself and die in my place upon the cross of Calvary." But how often do we kneel and say to the Holy Spirit, "Oh, eternal and infinite Spirit of God, I thank You for Your great love that led You to come into this world of sin and darkness and to seek me out and to follow me so patiently until

You did bring me to see my utter ruin and need of a Savior and to reveal to me my Lord and Savior, Jesus Christ, as just the Savior whom I need." Yet we owe our salvation just as truly to the love of the Spirit as we do to the love of the Father and the love of the Son.

If it had not been for the love of God the Father looking down upon me in my utter ruin and providing a perfect atonement for me in the death of His own Son on the cross of Calvary, I would have been in hell today. If it had not been for the love of Jesus Christ, the eternal Word of God, looking upon me in my utter ruin and in obedience to the Father, putting aside all the glory of heaven for all the shame of earth and taking my place, the place of the curse, upon the cross of Calvary and pouring out His life utterly for me, I would have been in hell today. But if it had not been for the love of the Holy Spirit, sent by the Father in answer to the prayer of the Son (see John 15:16), leading Him to seek me out in my utter blindness and ruin, I would have been in hell today. He followed me day after day, week after week, and year after year when I persistently turned a deaf ear to His pleadings, following me through paths of sin where it must have been agony for that holy One to go until at last I listened, and He opened my eyes to see my utter ruin and then revealed Jesus to me as just the Savior that would meet my every need and then enabled me to receive this Jesus as my own Savior. If it had not been for this patient, long-suffering, never-tiring, infinitely-tender love of the Holy Spirit, I would have been in hell today.

Oh, the Holy Spirit is not merely an influence or a power or an illumination but is a person just as real as God the Father or Jesus Christ His Son.

The personality of the Holy Spirit comes out in the Old Testament as truly as in the New, for we read in Nehemiah 9:20, "Thou gavest also thy good spirit to instruct them, and withheldest not thy manna from their mouth, and gavest them water for their thirst." Here both intelligence and goodness are ascribed to the Holy Spirit. There are some who tell us that while it is true the personality of the Holy Spirit is found in the New Testament, it is not found in the Old. However, it is certainly found in this passage. As a matter of course, the doctrine of the personality of the Holy Spirit is not as fully developed in the Old Testament as in the New, but the doctrine is there.

There is perhaps no passage in the entire Bible in which the personality of the Holy Spirit comes out more tenderly and touchingly than in the following: "And grieve not the holy Spirit of God, whereby ye are sealed unto the day of redemption" (Eph. 4:30). Here grief is ascribed to the Holy Spirit. The Holy Spirit is not a blind, impersonal influence or power that comes into our lives to illuminate, sanctify, and empower us. No, He is immeasurably more than that. He is a holy person who comes to dwell in our hearts, One who sees clearly every act we perform, every word we speak, every thought we entertain, even the most fleeting fancy that is allowed to pass through our minds. If there is anything in act or word or deed that is impure, unholy, unkind, selfish, mean, petty, or untrue, this infinitely Holy One is deeply grieved by it. I know of no thought that will help one more than this to lead a holy life and to walk softly in the presence of the Holy One.

How often a young man is kept back from yielding to the temptations that surround young manhood by the thought that if he should yield to the temptation that now assails him his holy mother might hear of it and would be grieved by it beyond expression. How often some young man has had his hand upon the door of some place of sin that he is about to enter and the thought has come to him, "If I should enter there, my mother might hear of it, and it would nearly kill her," and he has turned his back upon that door and gone away to lead a pure life that he might not grieve his mother.

There is One who is holier than any mother, One who is more sensitive against sin than the purest woman who ever walked this earth and who loves us as even no mother ever loved. This One dwells in our hearts, if we are really Christians, and He sees every act we do by day or under cover of the night. He hears every word we utter in public or in private. He sees every thought we entertain. He beholds every fancy and imagination that is permitted even a momentary lodging in our mind. If there is anything unholy, impure, selfish, mean, petty, unkind, harsh, unjust, or in any way evil in act or word or thought or fancy, He is grieved by it. If we will allow those words, "grieve not the Holy Spirit of God," to sink into our hearts and become the motto of our lives, they will keep us from many a sin. How often some thought or fancy has knocked for an entrance into my own mind and was about to find entertainment when the thought has come, "The Holy Spirit sees that thought and will be grieved by it," and that thought has gone.

Many acts that only a person can perform are ascribed to the Holy Spirit.

If we deny the personality of the Holy Spirit, many passages of Scripture become meaningless and absurd. For example, we read in 1 Corinthians 2:10, "But God hath revealed them unto us by his Spirit: for the Spirit searcheth all things, yea, the deep things of God." This passage sets before us the Holy Spirit not merely as an illumination whereby we are enabled to grasp the deep things of God but as a person who Himself searches the deep things of God and then reveals to us the precious discoveries which He has made.

We read in Revelation 2:7, "He that hath an ear, let him hear what the Spirit saith unto the churches; To him that overcometh will I give to eat of the tree of life, which is in the midst of the paradise of God." Here the Holy Spirit is set before us not merely as an impersonal enlightenment that comes to our mind but as a person who speaks and, out of the depths of His own wisdom, whispers into the ear of His listening servant the precious truth of God.

In Galatians 4:6 we read, "And because ye are sons, God hath sent forth the Spirit of his Son into your hearts, crying, Abba, Father." Here the Holy Spirit is represented as crying out in the heart of the individual believer. The Holy Spirit is not merely a divine influence producing in our own hearts the assurance of our sonship but one who cries out in our hearts, who bears witness together with our spirit that we are sons of God (Rom. 8:16).

The Holy Spirit is also represented in the Scripture as one who prays:

> *Likewise the Spirit also helpeth our infirmities: for we know not what we should pray for as we ought: but the Spirit itself maketh intercession for us with groanings which cannot be uttered.*   *(Rom. 8:26)*

It is plain from this passage that the Holy Spirit is not merely an influence that moves us to pray, not merely an illumination that teaches us how to pray, but a person who Himself prays in and through us.

There is wondrous comfort in the thought that every true believer has two divine persons praying for him. One is Jesus Christ, the Son who was once upon this earth, who knows all about our temptations, who can be touched with the feeling of our infirmities, and who is now ascended to the right hand of the Father and in that place of authority and power ever lives to make intercession for us. (See Hebrews 7:25; 1 John 2:1.) There is another person, just as divine as Christ, who walks by our side each day, who dwells in the innermost depths of our being, who knows our needs even as we do not know them ourselves, and who from these depths makes intercession to the Father for us. The position of the believer is indeed one of perfect security with these two divine persons praying for him.

We read in John 15:26, "But when the Comforter is come, whom I will send unto you from the Father, even the Spirit of truth, which proceedeth from the Father, he shall testify of me." Here the Holy Spirit is set before us as a person who gives His testimony to Jesus Christ not merely as an illumination that enables the believer to testify of Christ but as a person who Himself testifies. A clear distinction is drawn in this and in the following verse between the testimony of the Holy Spirit and the testimony of the believer to whom He has borne His witness, for we read, "And ye also shall bear witness, because ye have been with me from the beginning" (John 15:27). So there are two witnesses, the Holy Spirit bearing witness to the believer and the believer bearing witness to the world.

The Holy Spirit is also spoken of as a teacher: "But the Comforter, which is the Holy Ghost, whom the Father will send in My name, he shall teach you all things, and bring all things to your remembrance, whatsoever I have said unto you" (John 14:26). And in a similar way, we read,

I have yet many things to say unto you, but ye cannot bear them now. Howbeit when he, the Spirit of truth, is come, he will guide you into all truth: for he shall not speak of himself;

but whatsoever he shall hear, that shall he speak: and he will show you things to come. He shall glorify me: for he shall receive of mine, and shall show it unto you.

(John 16:12–14)

And in the Old Testament: "Thou gavest also thy good spirit to instruct them" (Neh. 9:20). In all these passages it is perfectly clear that the Holy Spirit is not a mere illumination that enables us to apprehend the truth but a person who comes to us to teach us day by day the truth of God. It is the privilege of the humblest believer in Jesus Christ not merely to have his mind illumined to comprehend the truth of God but to have a divine teacher to daily teach him the truth he needs to know. (See 1 John 2:20, 27.)

The Holy Spirit is also represented as the Leader and Guide of the children of God. We read in Romans 8:14, "For as many as are led by the Spirit of God they are the sons of God." He is not merely an influence that enables us to see the way that God would have us go, or merely a power that gives us strength to go that way, but a person who takes us by the hand and gently leads us on in the paths in which God would have us walk.

The Holy Spirit also has authority to command men in their service of Jesus Christ. We read of the apostle Paul and his companions,

Now when they had gone throughout Phrygia and the region of Galatia, and were forbidden of the Holy Ghost to preach the word in Asia, After they were come to Mysia, they

assayed to go into Bithynia: but the Spirit
suffered them not.   *(Acts 16:6–7)*

Here it is a person who takes the direction of the
conduct of Paul and his companions and a person
whose authority they recognized and to whom
they instantly submitted.

Further still than this the Holy Spirit is represented as the One who is the supreme authority
in the church, who calls men to work and appoints
them to office. We read in Acts 13:2, "As they
ministered to the Lord, and fasted, the Holy Ghost
said, Separate me Barnabas and Saul for the work
where unto I have called them." And: "Take heed
therefore unto yourselves, and to all the flock, over
the which the Holy Ghost hath made you overse-
ers, to feed the church of God, which he hath purchased with his own blood" (Acts 20:28). There
can be no doubt to a candid seeker after truth that
it is a person of divine majesty and sovereignty
who is here set before us.

From all the passages here quoted, it is evident that many acts that only a person can perform are ascribed to the Holy Spirit.

**An office is asserted by the Holy Spirit that can only be
asserted by a person.**

Our Savior says,

And I will pray the Father, and he shall give
you another Comforter, that he may abide
with you for ever; Even the Spirit of truth;
whom the world cannot receive, because it

20

*seeth him not, neither knoweth him: but ye
know him; for he dwelleth with you, and
shall be in you.*   *(John 14:16–17)*

Our Lord had announced to the disciples that He
was about to leave them. An awful sense of deso-
lation took possession of them. Sorrow filled their
hearts (see John 16:6) at the contemplation of
their loneliness and absolute helplessness when
Jesus would thus leave them alone. To comfort
them the Lord told them that they would not be
left alone, that in leaving them He was going to
the Father and that He would pray the Father and
would give them another Comforter to take the
place of Himself during His absence.

Is it possible that Jesus Christ could have
used such language if the other Comforter who
was coming to take His place was only an impersonal influence or power? Still more, is it possible
that Jesus could have said as He did in John 16:7,
"Nevertheless I tell you the truth: It is expedient
for you that I go away: for if I go not away, the
Comforter will not come unto you; but if I depart, I
will send him unto you," if this Comforter whom
He was to send was simply an impersonal influence or power? No, one divine person was going,
another person just as divine was coming to take
His place. For the disciples, it was necessary that
the One go to represent them before the Father
because another just as divine and sufficient was
coming to take His place. This promise of our Lord
and Savior of the coming of the other Comforter
and of His abiding with us is the greatest and best

of all for the present dispensation. This is the promise of the Father (see Acts 1:4), the promise of promises. We will take it up again when we come to study the names of the Holy Spirit.

A treatment is asserted by the Holy Spirit that could only be asserted by a person.

We read in Isaiah 63:10 (ASV), "But they rebelled and grieved his holy Spirit: therefore he was turned to be their enemy, and himself fought against them." Here we are told that the Holy Spirit is rebelled against and grieved. (Compare Ephesians 4:30.) Only a person, and only a person of authority, can be rebelled against. Only a person can be grieved. You cannot grieve a mere influence or power.

In Hebrews we read,

> *Of how much sorer punishment, suppose ye,*
> *shall he be thought worthy, who hath trod-*
> *den under foot the Son of God, and hath*
> *counted the blood of the covenant, wherewith*
> *he was sanctified, an unholy thing, and hath*
> *done despite unto the Spirit of grace?*
> *(Heb. 10:29)*

Here we are told that the Holy Spirit is "done despite unto" (treated with contempt). There is but one kind of entity in the universe that can be treated with contempt (or insulted) and that is a person. It is absurd to think of treating an influence or a power or any kind of being except a person with contempt.

22

We also read, "But Peter said, Ananias, why hath Satan filled thine heart to lie to the Holy Ghost, and to keep back part of the price of the land?" (Acts 5:3). Here we have the Holy Spirit represented as one who can be lied to. One cannot lie to anything but a person.

In Matthew we read,

> Wherefore I say unto you, All manner of sin and blasphemy shall be forgiven unto men: but the blasphemy against the Holy Ghost shall not be forgiven unto men. And whosoever speaketh a word against the Son of man, it shall be forgiven him: but whosoever speaketh against the Holy Ghost, it shall not be forgiven him, neither in this world, neither in the world to come.   (Matt. 12:31–32)

Here we are told that the Holy Spirit is blasphemed against. It is impossible to blaspheme anything but a person. If the Holy Spirit is not a person, it certainly cannot be a more serious and decisive sin to blaspheme Him than it is to blaspheme the Son of man, our Lord and Savior, Jesus Christ Himself.

Here then we have four distinctive and decisive lines of proof that the Holy Spirit is a person. Theoretically most of us believe this, but do we, in our real thoughts of Him and in our practical attitudes towards Him, treat Him as if He were indeed a person?

At the close of an address on the personality of the Holy Spirit at a Bible conference some years ago, one who had been a church member many years, a member of one of the most orthodox of our modern denominations, said to me, "I never thought of the Holy Spirit before as a person." Doubtless this Christian woman had often sung,

> Praise God from whom all blessings flow,
> > Praise Him all creatures here below,
> Praise Him above, ye heavenly host,
> > Praise Father, Son, and Holy Ghost.

Doubtless she had often sung,

> Glory be to the Father,
> > and to the Son,
> > and to the Holy Ghost,
> As it was in the beginning,
> > is now, and ever shall be,
> World without end,
> > Amen, Amen.

However, it is one thing to sing words; it is quite another thing to realize the meaning of what we sing. If this Christian woman had been questioned in regard to her doctrine, she would doubtless have said that she believed that there were three persons in the Godhead: Father, Son, and Holy Spirit. But a theological confession is one thing; a practical realization of the truth we confess is quite another. So the question is altogether necessary, no matter how orthodox you may be in your doctrinal statements: Do you indeed regard the Holy Spirit as real a person as Jesus Christ, as loving and wise and strong, as worthy of your confidence and love and surrender as Jesus Christ Himself?

The Holy Spirit came into this world to be to the disciples of our Lord after His departure, and to us, what Jesus Christ had been to them during the days of His personal companionship with them. (See John 14:16–17.) Is He that to you? Do you know Him? Every week in your life you hear the apostolic benediction, "The grace of the Lord Jesus Christ, and the love of God, and the communion of the Holy Ghost be with you all" (2 Cor. 13:14), but while you hear it, do you take in the significance of it? Do you know the communion of the Holy Ghost? The fellowship of the Holy Ghost? The partnership of the Holy Ghost? The comradeship of the Holy Ghost? The intimate personal friendship of the Holy Ghost?

Here lies the whole secret of a real Christian life, a life of liberty and joy and power and fullness. To have as one's ever-present friend, and to be conscious that one has as his ever-present friend, the Holy Spirit and to surrender one's life in all its departments entirely to His control—this is true Christian living. The doctrine of the personality of the Holy Spirit is as distinctive of the religion that Jesus taught as the doctrines of the deity and the atonement of Jesus Christ Himself. But it is not enough to believe the doctrine; one must know the Holy Spirit Himself. The whole purpose of this chapter (God help me to say it reverently) is to introduce you to my friend, the Holy Spirit.

Chapter 2

The Deity of the Holy Spirit

In the preceding chapter we have seen clearly that the Holy Spirit is a person, but what sort of a person is He? Is He a finite person or an infinite person? Is He God? This question also is plainly answered in the Bible. There are in the Scriptures of the Old and New Testaments five distinct and decisive pieces of evidence of the deity of the Holy Spirit.

Each of the four distinctively divine attributes is ascribed to the Holy Spirit.

What are the distinctively divine attributes? Eternity, omnipresence, omniscience, and omnipotence. All of these are ascribed to the Holy Spirit in the Bible. We find eternity ascribed to the Holy Spirit in Hebrews 9:14: "How much more shall the blood of Christ, who through the eternal Spirit offered himself without spot to God, purge your conscience from dead works to serve the living God?"

Omnipresence is ascribed to the Holy Spirit in the following verses:

Whither shall I go from thy spirit? Or whither shall I flee from thy presence? If I ascend up into heaven, thou art there: if I make my bed in hell, behold, thou art there. If I take the wings of the morning, and dwell in the uttermost parts of the sea; even there shall thy hand lead me, and thy right hand shall hold me.   *(Ps. 139:7–10)*

Omniscience is ascribed to the Holy Spirit in several passages. For example, we read the following passages from Scripture:

But God hath revealed them unto us by his Spirit: for the Spirit searcheth all things, yea, the deep things of God. For what man knoweth the things of a man, save the spirit of man which is in him? even so the things of God knoweth no man, but the Spirit of God.   *(1 Cor. 2:10–11)*

But the Comforter, which is the Holy Ghost, whom the Father will send in my name, he shall teach you all things, and bring all things to your remembrance, whatsoever I have said unto you.   *(John 14:26)*

I have yet many things to say unto you, but ye cannot bear them now. Howbeit when he, the Spirit of truth, is come, he will guide you into all truth: for he shall not speak of himself; but whatsoever he shall hear, that shall he speak: and he will show you things to come.   *(John 16:12–13)*

We find omnipotence ascribed to the Holy Spirit in Luke 1:35:

And the angel answered and said unto her, The Holy Ghost shall come upon thee, and the power of the Highest shall overshadow thee: therefore also that holy thing which shall be born of thee shall be called the Son of God.

Three distinctively divine works are ascribed to the Holy Spirit.

When we think of God and His work, the first work of which we always think is that of creation. In the Scriptures creation is ascribed to the Holy Spirit. We read in Job 33:4, "The spirit of God hath made me, and the breath of the Almighty hath given me life." We read still again in Psalm 104:30, "Thou sendest forth thy spirit, they are created: and thou renewest the face of the earth." The activity of the Spirit is referred to in connection with the description of creation in the first chapter of Genesis. (See Genesis 1:1–3.)

The impartation of life is also a divine work, and this is ascribed in the Scriptures to the Holy Spirit. We read in John 6:63, "It is the spirit that quickeneth; the flesh profiteth nothing." We read also in Romans 8:11, "But if the Spirit of him that raised up Jesus from the dead dwell in you, he that raised up Christ from the dead shall also quicken your mortal bodies by his Spirit that dwelleth in you." In the description of the creation of man in Genesis 2:7, it is the breath of God, that is the Holy Spirit, who imparts life to man, and man becomes a living soul. The exact words are, "And the LORD God formed man of the dust of the ground, and breathed into his nostrils the breath of life; and man became a living soul." Although the Holy Spirit as a person does not come out distinctly in this early reference to Him in Genesis 2:7, this passage interpreted in the light of the fuller revelation of the New Testament clearly refers to the Holy Spirit because the Greek word which is rendered "spirit" means "breath."

The authorship of divine prophecies is also ascribed to the Holy Spirit. We read in 2 Peter 1:21, "For the prophecy came not in old time by the will of man: but holy men of God spake as they were moved by the Holy Ghost." Even in the Old Testament, there is a reference to the Holy Spirit as the author of prophecy. We read in 2 Samuel 23:2–3,

> The Spirit of the LORD spake by me, and his word was in my tongue. The God of Israel said, the Rock of Israel spake to me, He that ruleth over men must be just, ruling in the fear of God.

So we see that the three distinctly divine works—creation, the impartation of life, and prophecy—are ascribed to the Holy Spirit.

Statements which in the Old Testament distinctly name the LORD or Jehovah as their subject are applied to the Holy Spirit in the New Testament. Thus, the Holy Spirit occupies the position of deity in New Testament thought.

A striking illustration of this is found in a comparison of a passage in Isaiah and one in Acts.

> *Mine eyes have seen the King, the LORD of hosts...And He said, Go, and tell this people, Hear ye indeed, but understand not; and see ye indeed, but perceive not. Make the heart of this people fat, and make their ears heavy, and shut their eyes; lest they see with their eyes, and hear with their ears, and understand with their heart, and convert, and be healed.* (Isaiah 6:5, 9–10).

In verse five we are told that it was Jehovah (whenever the word LORD is spelled in capitals in the Old Testament, it stands for Jehovah in the Hebrew) whom Isaiah saw and who speaks. But in Acts there is a reference to this statement of Isaiah's, and whereas in Isaiah we are told it is Jehovah who speaks, in the reference in Acts we are told that it was the Holy Spirit who was the speaker. The passage in Acts reads as follows:

> *And when they agreed not among themselves, they departed, after that Paul had spoken one word, Well spake the Holy Ghost by Esaias the prophet unto our fathers, Saying, Go unto this people, and say, Hearing ye shall hear, and shall not understand; and*

seeing ye shall see and not perceive: For the heart of this people is waxed gross, and their ears are dull of hearing, and their eyes have they closed; lest they should see with their eyes, and hear with their ears, and understand with their heart, and should be converted, and I should heal them. (Acts 28:25–27)

So we see that what is distinctly ascribed to Jehovah in the Old Testament is ascribed to the Holy Spirit in the New; thus, the Holy Spirit is identified with Jehovah. It is a noteworthy fact that in the gospel of John, chapter twelve verses thirty-eight to forty-one, where another reference to this passage in Isaiah is made, this same passage is ascribed to Christ (note carefully the forty-first verse). So in different parts of Scripture, we have the same passage referred to Jehovah, referred to the Holy Spirit, and referred to Jesus Christ. May we not find the explanation of this in the threefold "Holy" of the angelic cry in Isaiah 6:3, where we read, "And one cried unto another, and said, Holy, holy, holy, is the LORD of hosts: the whole earth is full of his glory." In this we have a distinct suggestion of the tri-personality of the Jehovah of Hosts and hence the propriety of the threefold application of the vision. A further suggestion of this tri-personality of Jehovah of Hosts is found in Isaiah 6:8 where the Lord is represented as saying, "Whom shall I send, and who will go for us?"

Another striking illustration of the application of passages which in the Old Testament distinctly name Jehovah as their subject to the Holy Spirit in the New Testament is found in Exodus 16:7. Here we read, "And in the morning, then ye shall see the glory of the LORD; for that he heareth your murmurings against the LORD: and what are we that ye murmur against us?" Here the murmuring of the children of Israel is distinctly said to be against Jehovah. But in Hebrews 3:7–9, where this instance is referred to, we read,

> *Wherefore as the Holy Ghost saith, To day if ye will hear his voice, harden not your hearts, as in the provocation, in the day of temptation in the wilderness: When your fathers tempted me, proved me, and saw my works forty years.*

The murmurings which Moses says were against Jehovah, in the book of Exodus, we are told in Hebrews were against the Holy Spirit. This leaves it beyond question that the Holy Spirit occupies the position of Jehovah (or Deity) in the New Testament. (Compare Psalm 95:8–11.)

The name of the Holy Spirit is coupled with that of God in a way it would be impossible for a reverent and thoughtful mind to couple the name of any finite being with that of the Deity.

We have an illustration of this in 1 Corinthians:

> *Now there are diversities of gifts, but the same Spirit: And there are differences of administrations, but the same Lord. And there are diversities of operations, but it is the same God which worketh all in all.* (1 Cor. 12:4–6)

Here we find God and the Lord and the Spirit associated together in a relation of equality that would be shocking to contemplate if the Spirit were a finite being. We have a still more striking illustration of this in Matthew 28:19: "Go ye therefore, and teach all nations, baptizing them in the name of the Father, and of the Son, and of the Holy Ghost." What person who had grasped the biblical conception of God the Father would think for a moment of coupling the name of the Holy Spirit with that of the Father in this way if the Holy Spirit were a finite being, even the most exalted of angelic beings?

Another striking illustration is found in 2 Corinthians 13:14: "The grace of the Lord Jesus Christ, and the love of God, and the communion of the Holy Ghost, be with you all. Amen." Can anyone ponder these words and catch anything like their real importance without seeing clearly that it would be impossible to couple the name of the Holy Spirit with that of God the Father in the way in which it is coupled in this verse unless the Holy Spirit were Himself a divine being?

The Holy Spirit is called God.

The final and decisive proof of the deity of the Holy Spirit is found in the fact that He is called God in the New Testament. We read in Acts 5:3–4,

But Peter said, Ananias, why hath Satan filled thine heart to lie to the Holy Ghost, and to keep back part of the price of the land? Whiles it remained, was it not thine own? and after it was sold, was it not in

33

thine own power? why hast thou conceived this thing in thine heart? thou hast not lied unto men but unto God.

In the first part of this passage, we are told that Ananias lied to the Holy Spirit. When this is further explained, we are told it was not to men but to God that he had lied in lying to the Holy Spirit; in other words, the Holy Spirit to whom he lied is called God.

To sum it all up, by the ascription of all the distinctively divine attributes and several distinctly divine works, by comparing statements which clearly name Jehovah, the Lord, or God as their subject in the Old Testament to the Holy Spirit in the New Testament, by coupling the name of the Holy Spirit with that of God in a way that would be impossible to couple that of any finite being with that of deity, and by plainly calling the Holy Spirit God—in all these unmistakable ways, God in His own Word distinctly proclaims that the Holy Spirit is a divine person.

Chapter 3

The Holy Spirit's Distinction from the Father and from His Son

We have seen thus far that the Holy Spirit is a person and a divine person. And now another question arises: Is He, as a divine person, separate and distinct from the Father and from the Son? One who carefully studies the New Testament statements cannot but discover that beyond a question He is. We read in Luke 3:21–22,

> Now when all the people were baptized, it came to pass, that Jesus also being baptized, and praying, the heaven was opened, and the Holy Ghost descended in a bodily shape like a dove upon him, and a voice came from heaven, which said, Thou art my beloved Son; in thee I am well pleased.

Here the clearest possible distinction is drawn between Jesus Christ, who was on earth, and the Father, who spoke to Him from heaven as one person speaks to another person, and the Holy Spirit, who descended in a bodily form as a dove from the Father (who was speaking) to the Son (to whom He was speaking) and rested upon the Son as a person separate and distinct from Himself.

We see a clear distinction drawn between the name of the Father and that of the Son and that of the Holy Spirit in Matthew 28:19 where we read, "Go ye therefore, and teach all nations, baptizing them in the name of the Father, and of the Son, and of the Holy Ghost." The distinction of the Holy Spirit from the Father and the Son comes out again with exceeding clearness in John 14:16: "And I will pray the Father, and he shall give you another Comforter, that he may abide with you forever." Here we see the one person, the Son, praying to another person, the Father, and the Father to whom He is praying giving another person, another Comforter, in answer to the prayer of the second person, the Son. If words mean anything, and certainly in the Bible they mean what they say, there can be no mistaking that the Father and the Son and the Spirit are three distinct and separate persons.

Again in John 16:7, a clear distinction is drawn between Jesus who goes away to the Father and the Holy Spirit who comes from the Father to take His place. Jesus says, "Nevertheless I tell you the truth; It is expedient for you that I go away: for if I go not away, the Comforter will not come unto you; but if I depart, I will send him unto you." A similar distinction is drawn in Acts 2:33, where we read, "Therefore [Jesus] being by the right hand of God exalted, and having received of the Father the promise of the Holy Ghost, he hath shed forth this, which ye now see and hear." In this passage, the clearest possible distinction is drawn between the Son exalted to the right hand of the Father and the Father to whose right hand He is exalted and the Holy Spirit whom the Son receives from the Father and sheds forth upon the church.

To sum it all up, again and again the Bible draws the clearest possible distinction between the three persons, the Holy Spirit, the Father, and the Son. They are three separate personalities, having mutual relations to one another, acting upon one another, speaking of or to one another, applying the pronouns of the second and third persons to one another.

Chapter 4

The Subordination of the Spirit to the Father and to the Son

From the fact that the Holy Spirit is a divine person, it does not follow that the Holy Spirit is in every sense equal to the Father. While the Scriptures teach that in Jesus Christ dwelt all the fullness of the Godhead in a bodily form (Col. 2:9) and that He was so truly and fully divine that He could say, "I and my Father are one" (John 10:30) and "he that hath seen me hath seen the Father" (John 14:9), they also teach with equal clearness that Jesus Christ was not equal to the Father in every respect but subordinate to the Father in many ways.

In a similar way, the Scriptures teach us that though the Holy Spirit is a divine person, He is subordinate to the Father and to the Son. We are taught that the Holy Spirit is sent by the Father and in the name of the Son. Jesus declares very clearly,

> *But the Comforter, which is the Holy Ghost, whom the Father will send in my name, he*

shall teach you all things, and bring all
things to your remembrance, whatsoever I
have said unto you.   *(John 14:26)*

In John 15:26 we are told that it is Jesus who sends the Spirit from the Father. The exact words are, "But when the Comforter is come, whom I will send unto you from the Father, even the Spirit of truth, which proceedeth from the Father, he shall testify of me." Just as we are elsewhere taught that Jesus Christ was sent by the Father (see John 6:29; 8:29, 42), we are here taught that the Holy Spirit in turn is sent by Jesus Christ.

The subordination of the Holy Spirit to the Father and the Son comes out also in the fact that He derives some of His names from the Father and from the Son. We read in Romans 8:9, "But ye are not in the flesh, but in the Spirit, if so be that the Spirit of God dwell in you. Now if any man have not the Spirit of Christ, he is none of his." Here we have two names of the Spirit, one derived from His relation to the Father, "the Spirit of God," and the other derived from His relation to the Son, "the Spirit of Christ." In Acts 16:7 (RV), He is spoken of as "the Spirit of Jesus."

The subordination of the Spirit to the Son is also seen in the fact that the Holy Spirit speaks not from Himself but speaks the words which He hears. We read in John,

Howbeit when he, the Spirit of truth, is
come, he will guide you into all truth: for he
shall not speak of himself; but whatsoever he

*shall hear, that shall he speak: and he will
show you things to come.   (John 16:13)*

In a similar way, Jesus said of Himself, "My doctrine is not mine, but his that sent me" (John 7:16; see also 8:26, 40).

The subordination of the Spirit to the Son comes out again in the clearly revealed fact that it is the work of the Holy Spirit not to glorify Himself but to glorify Christ. Jesus says in John 16:14, "He shall glorify me: for he shall receive of mine, and shall show it unto you." In a similar way, Christ sought not His own glory, but the glory of Him that sent Him, that is the Father. (See John 7:18.)

From all these passages, it is evident that the Holy Spirit in His present work, while possessed of all the attributes of deity, is subordinated to the Father and to the Son. On the other hand, we shall see later that in His earthly life, Jesus lived and taught and worked in the power of the Holy Spirit.

Chapter 5

The Person and Work of the Holy Spirit as Revealed in His Names

At least twenty-five different names are used in the Old and New Testaments in speaking of the Holy Spirit. There is the deepest significance in these names. By the careful study of them, we find a wonderful revelation of the person and work of the Holy Spirit.

1. THE SPIRIT

The simplest name by which the Holy Spirit is mentioned in the Bible is that which stands at the head of this paragraph: "The Spirit." This name is also used as the basis of other names, so we begin our study with this. The Greek and Hebrew words so translated mean literally, "Breath" or "Wind." Both thoughts are in the name as applied to the Holy Spirit.

The thought of *breath* is brought out in John 20:22 where we read, "And when he had said this, he breathed on them, and saith unto them, Receive ye the Holy Ghost." It is also suggested in

Genesis 2:7: "And the LORD God formed man of the dust of the ground, and breathed into his nostrils the breath of life; and man became a living soul." This becomes more evident when we compare this with Psalm 104:30: "Thou sendest forth thy spirit, they are created: and thou renewest the face of the earth," and with Job 33:4: "The spirit of God hath made me, and the breath of the Almighty hath given me life." What is the significance of this name from the standpoint of these passages? It is that the Spirit is the outbreathing of God, His inmost life going forth in a personal form to enliven.

When we receive the Holy Spirit, we receive the inmost life of God Himself to dwell in a personal way in us. When we really grasp this thought, it is overwhelming in its solemnity. Just stop and think what it means to have the inmost life of that infinite and eternal being whom we call God dwelling in a personal way in you. How solemn and how awesome and yet unspeakably glorious life becomes when we realize this.

The thought of the Holy Spirit as the Wind is brought out in the following Scripture passage.

That which is born of the flesh is flesh; and that which is born of the Spirit is spirit. Marvel not that I said unto thee, Ye must be born again. The wind bloweth where it listeth, and thou hearest the sound thereof, but canst not tell whence it cometh, and whither it goeth: so is every one that is born of the Spirit. *(John 3:6–8)*

In the Greek, it is the same word that is translated in one part of this passage "Spirit" and the other part of the passage "wind." And it would seem as if the word ought to be translated the same way in both parts of the passage. It would then read, "That which is born of the flesh is flesh and that which is born of the 'Wind' is wind. Marvel not that I said unto thee, Ye must be born again. The wind bloweth where it listeth and thou hearest the sound thereof, but canst not tell whence it cometh or whither it goeth: so is everyone that is born of the 'Wind.'" The full significance of this name as applied to the Holy Spirit (or Holy Wind) may be beyond us to fathom, but we can see at least this much of its meaning through the following sections.

The Spirit, like the wind, is sovereign.

"The wind bloweth where it listeth" (John 3:8). You cannot dictate to the wind. It does as it wills. Just so with the Holy Spirit—He is sovereign—we cannot dictate to Him. He divides "to every man severally as he will" (1 Cor. 12:11). When the wind is blowing from the north, you may long to have it blow from the south, but cry as noisily as you may to the wind, "Blow from the south," it will keep right on blowing from the north. While you cannot dictate to the wind, while it blows as it will, you may learn the laws that govern the wind's motions. By bringing yourself into harmony with these laws, you can get the wind to do your work. You can erect your windmill so that, whichever way the wind blows from, the wheels will turn and the wind will grind your grain or pump your water. Just so, while we cannot dictate to the Holy Spirit, we can learn the laws of His operations. By bringing ourselves into harmony with those laws, above all by submitting our wills absolutely to His sovereign will, the sovereign Spirit of God will work through us and accomplish His own glorious work by our instrumentality.

The Spirit like the wind is invisible but none the less perceptible and real and mighty.

You hear the sound of the wind (see John 3:8), but the wind itself you never see. You hear the voice of the Spirit, but He Himself is ever invisible. (The word translated "sound" in John 3:8 is the word which is translated "voice" elsewhere in Scripture and here in other versions.) We not only hear the voice of the wind, but we see its mighty effects. We feel the breath of the wind upon our cheeks; we see the dust and the leaves blowing before the wind; we see the vessels at sea driven swiftly towards their ports; but the wind itself remains invisible. Just so it is with the Spirit; we feel His breath upon our souls and see the mighty things He does, but Him we do not see. He is invisible, but He is real and perceptible.

I will never forget a solemn hour in Chicago Avenue Church in Chicago. Dr. W. W. White was making a farewell address before going to India to work among the students there. Suddenly, without any apparent warning, the place was filled with an awesome and glorious Presence. To me it was very real, but the question arose in my mind, "Is this merely subjective, just a feeling of my own, or is there an objective Presence here?" After the meeting was over, I asked different people whether they were conscious of anything and found that at the same point in the meeting they too, though they saw no one, became distinctly conscious of an overwhelming Presence, the Presence of the Holy Spirit. Though many years have passed, there are those who speak of that hour to this day.

On another occasion in my own home in Chicago, when kneeling in prayer with an intimate friend, it seemed as if an unseen and awesome Presence entered the room as we prayed. I realized what Eliphaz meant when he said, "Then a spirit passed before my face; the hair of my flesh stood up" (Job 4:15). The moment was overwhelming but as glorious as it was awesome.

These are but two illustrations of which many might be given. None of us have seen the Holy Spirit at any time, but of His presence we have been distinctly conscious again and again and again. His mighty power we have witnessed, and His reality we cannot doubt. There are those who tell us that they do not believe in anything which they cannot see. Not one of them has ever seen the wind, but they all believe in the wind. They have felt the wind, and they have seen its effects. Just so we, beyond a question, have felt the mighty presence of the Spirit and witnessed His mighty workings.

The Spirit, like the wind, is inscrutable.

"Thou...canst not tell whence it cometh, and whither it goeth" (John 3:8). Nothing in nature is more mysterious than the wind. Even more mysterious still is the Holy Spirit in His operations. We hear of how suddenly and unexpectedly in widely separated communities He begins to work His mighty work. Doubtless there are hidden reasons why He thus begins His work, but often these reasons are completely undiscoverable by us. We know not where He comes from or where He goes. We cannot tell where next He will display His mighty and gracious power.

The Spirit, like the wind, is indispensable.

Without wind, that is "air in motion," there is no life, and so Jesus says, "Verily, verily, I say unto thee, Except a man be born of water and of the Spirit, he cannot enter into the kingdom of God" (John 3:5). If the wind should absolutely cease to blow for a single hour, most of the life on this earth would cease to be. Time and again when the health reports of the different cities of the United States are issued, it has been found that the five healthiest cities in the United States were five cities located on the Great Lakes. Many have been surprised at this report when they have visited some of these cities and found that they were far from being the cleanest cities or the most sanitary in their general arrangement. Yet year after year this fact has been reported. The explanation is simply this: it is the wind blowing from the lakes that has brought life and health to the cities. Just so, when the Spirit ceases to blow in any heart or any church or any community, death ensues, but when the Spirit blows steadily upon the individual or the church or the community, there is abounding spiritual life and health.

Closely related to the foregoing thought, like the wind, the Holy Spirit is life giving.

This thought comes out again and again in the Scriptures. For example, we read in John 6:63 (ASV), "It is the spirit that giveth life," and in 2 Corinthians 3:6, we read, "The letter killeth, but the spirit giveth life." Perhaps the most suggestive passage on this point is Ezekiel 37:8–10. (Compare John 3:5.)

> *And when I beheld, lo, the sinews and the flesh came up upon them, and the skin covered them above: but there was no breath in them. Then said he unto me, Prophesy unto the wind, prophesy, son of man, and say to the wind, Thus saith the Lord GOD; Come from the four winds, O breath, and breathe upon these slain, that they may live. So I prophesied as he commanded me, and the breath came into them, and they lived, and stood upon their feet, an exceeding great army.*

Israel, in the prophet's vision, was only bones, very many and very dry (vv. 2, 11), until the prophet proclaimed to them the word of God. Then there was a noise and a shaking and the bones came together, bone joined to bone, and the sinews and the flesh came upon the bones. Still there was no life, but when the wind blew the breath of God's Spirit, then they "stood up upon their feet an exceeding great army."

All life in the individual believer, the teacher, the preacher, and the church is the Holy Spirit's work. You will sometimes make the acquaintance of a man, and as you hear him talk and observe his conduct, you are repelled and disgusted. Everything about him declares that he is a dead man, a moral corpse, and not only dead but rapidly decaying. You get away from him as quickly as you can. Months afterwards you meet him again. You hesitate to speak to him; you want to get out of his very presence. But you do speak to him, and he has not uttered many sentences before you notice a marvelous change. His conversation is sweet and wholesome and uplifting; everything about his manner is attractive and delightful. You soon discover that the man's whole conduct and life has been transformed. He is no longer a decaying corpse but a living child of God. What has happened? The Wind of God has blown upon him; he has received the Holy Spirit, the Holy Wind.

Some quiet Sabbath day you visit a church. Everything about the outward appointments of the church are all that could be desired. There is an attractive meeting-house, an expensive organ, a gifted choir, a scholarly preacher. The service is well arranged, but you have not been long at the gathering before you are forced to see that there is no life, that it is all form and that there is nothing really being accomplished for God or for man. You go away with a heavy heart. Months afterwards you have occasion to visit the church again. The outward appointments of the church are much as they were before, but the service has not proceeded far before you note a great difference. There is a new power in the singing, a new spirit in the prayer, a new grip in the preaching; everything about the church is teeming with the life of God. What has happened? The Wind of God has blown upon that church; the Holy Spirit, the Holy Wind, has come.

You go some day to hear a preacher of whose abilities you have heard great reports. As he stands up to preach, you soon learn that almost all of what has been said in praise of his abilities has been from the merely intellectual and rhetorical standpoint. His diction is faultless, his style beautiful, his logic unimpeachable, his orthodoxy beyond criticism. It is an intellectual treat to listen to him. Yet after all, as he preaches, you cannot avoid a feeling of sadness for there is no real grip, no real power, indeed, no reality of any kind in the man's preaching. You go away with a heavy heart at the thought of this waste of magnificent abilities. Months, perhaps years, pass by. You again find yourself listening to this celebrated preacher, but what a change! The same faultless diction, the same beautiful style, the same unimpeachable logic, the same skillful articulation, the same sound orthodoxy, but now there is something more. There is reality, life, grip, and power in the preaching. Men and women sit breathless as he speaks, sinners bowed with tears of contrition, pricked to their hearts with conviction of sin. Men and women and boys and girls renounce their selfishness, their sin, and their worldliness and accept Jesus Christ and surrender their lives to Him. What has happened? The Wind of God has blown upon that man. He has been filled with the Holy Wind.

Like the wind, the Holy Spirit is irresistible.

We read in Acts 1:8,

> *But ye shall receive power, after that the Holy Ghost is come upon you: and ye shall be witnesses unto me both in Jerusalem, and in all Judaea, and in Samaria, and unto the uttermost parts of the earth.*

When this promise of our Lord was fulfilled in Stephen, we read, "And they were not able to resist the wisdom and the spirit by which he spake" (Acts 6:10). A man filled with the Holy Spirit is transformed into a cyclone. What can stand before the wind? When St. Cloud, Minnesota, was visited with a cyclone years ago, the wind picked up loaded freight cars and carried them off the track. It wrenched an iron bridge from its foundations, twisted it together, and hurled it away. When a cyclone later visited St. Louis, Missouri, it cut off telegraph poles a foot in diameter as if they had been pipe stems. It cut off enormous trees close to the root, and it cut off the corner of brick buildings where it passed as though they had been cut by a knife. Nothing could stand before it, and so, nothing can stand before a Spirit-filled preacher of the Word.

None can resist the wisdom and the Spirit by which he speaks. The Wind of God took possession of Charles G. Finney, an obscure country lawyer, and sent him through New York state, then through New England, then through England, mowing down strong men by his resistless, Spirit-given logic. One night in Rochester, scores of lawyers, led by the justice of the Court of Appeals, filed out of the pews and bowed in the aisles and yielded their lives to God.

The Wind of God took possession of D. L. Moody, an uneducated young businessman in Chicago. In the power of this resistless Wind, men, women, and young people were mowed down before his words, brought in humble confession and renunciation of sin to the feet of Jesus Christ, and filled with the life of God. They have been the pillars in the churches of Great Britain and throughout the world ever since. The great need today in individuals, in churches, and in preachers is that the Wind of God blow upon us.

Much of the difficulty that many find with John 3:5, "Jesus answered, Verily, verily, I say unto thee, Except a man be born of water and of the Spirit, he cannot enter into the kingdom of God," would disappear if we would only bear in mind that "Spirit" means "Wind" and translate the verse literally all through: "Except a man be born of water and Wind [there is no "the" in the original], he cannot enter the kingdom of God." The thought would then seem to be, "Except a man be born of the cleansing and quickening power of the Spirit [or else of the cleansing Word— compare John 15:3; Ephesians 5:26; James 1:18; 1 Peter 1:23—and the quickening power of the Holy Spirit]."

2. THE SPIRIT OF GOD

The Holy Spirit is frequently spoken of in the Bible as the Spirit of God. For example: "Know ye not that ye are the temple of God, and that the Spirit of God dwelleth in you?" (1 Cor. 3:16). In this name we have the same essential thought as in the former name but with this addition, that His divine origin, nature, and power are emphasized. He is not merely "The Wind" as seen in number one above, but "The Wind of God."

3. THE SPIRIT OF JEHOVAH

This name of the Holy Spirit is used in Isaiah 11:2 (ASV): "And the Spirit of Jehovah shall rest upon him." The thought of the name is, of course, essentially the same as the preceding with the exception that God is here thought of as the Covenant God of Israel. He is thus spoken of in the connection in which the name is found, and, of course, the Bible, following that unerring accuracy that it always exhibits in its use of the different names for God, in this connection speaks of the Spirit as the Spirit of Jehovah and not merely as the Spirit of God.

4. THE SPIRIT OF THE LORD JEHOVAH

The Holy Spirit is called the Spirit of the Lord Jehovah in Isaiah 61:1 (ASV):

The Spirit of the Lord Jehovah is upon me; because Jehovah hath anointed me to preach good tidings unto the meek; he hath sent me to bind up the broken-hearted, to proclaim liberty to the captives....

The Holy Spirit is here spoken of not merely as the Spirit of Jehovah but as the Spirit of the Lord Jehovah because of the relation in which God Himself is spoken of in this connection. He is spoken of as not merely Jehovah, the covenant God of Israel, but as Jehovah, Israel's Lord as well as their covenant-keeping God. This name of the Spirit is even more expressive than the name: "The Spirit of God."

5. THE SPIRIT OF THE LIVING GOD

The Holy Spirit is called "The Spirit of the living God" in 2 Corinthians 3:3:

Forasmuch as ye are manifestly declared to be the epistle of Christ ministered by us, written not with ink, but with the Spirit of the living God; not in tables of stone, but in fleshly tables of the heart.

What is the significance of this name? It is made clear by the context. The apostle Paul is drawing a contrast between the Word of God written with ink on parchment and the Word of God written on "fleshly tables of the heart" by the Holy Spirit. In this connection, the Holy Spirit is called "the Spirit of the living God" because He makes God a living reality in our personal experience instead of a mere intellectual concept.

There are many who believe in God and who are perfectly orthodox in their conception of God, but, after all, God is to them only an intellectual theological proposition. It is the work of the Holy Spirit to make God something vastly more than a theological notion, no matter how orthodox. He is the Spirit of the living God, and it is His work to make God a living God to us, a being whom we know, with whom we have personal acquaintance, a being more real to us than the most intimate human friend we have. Have you a real God? Well, you may have. The Holy Spirit is the Spirit of the living God, and He is able and ready to give to you a living God, to make God real in your personal experience.

There are many who have a God who once lived and acted and spoke, a God who lived and acted at the creation of the universe, who perhaps lived and acted in the days of Moses and Elijah and Jesus Christ and the apostles, but who no longer lives and acts. If He exists at all, He has withdrawn Himself from any active part in nature or the history of man. He created nature and gave it its laws and powers and now leaves it to run itself.

He created man and endowed him with his various faculties but has now left him to work out his own destiny. They may go further than this; they may believe in a God who spoke to Abraham and to Moses and to David and to Isaiah and to Jesus and to the apostles but who speaks no longer. We may read in the Bible what He spoke to these various men, but we cannot expect Him to speak to us.

In contrast with these, it is the work of the Holy Spirit, the Spirit of the living God, to give us to know a God who lives and acts and speaks today, a God who is ready to come as near to us as He came to Abraham, to Moses, to Isaiah, to the apostles, or to Jesus Himself. Not that He has any new revelations to make for He guided the apostles into all the truth (see John 16:13), but though there has been a complete revelation of God's truth made in the Bible, still God lives today and will speak to us as directly as He spoke to His chosen ones of old. Happy is the man who knows the Holy Spirit as the Spirit of the living God, and who, consequently, has a real God, a God who lives today, a God upon whom he can depend today to undertake for him, a God with whom he enjoys intimate personal fellowship, a God to whom he may raise his voice in prayer and who speaks back to him.

6. THE SPIRIT OF CHRIST

"But ye are not in the flesh, but in the Spirit, if so be that the Spirit of God dwell in you. Now if any man have not the Spirit of Christ, he is none

55

of his" (Rom. 8:9). The Holy Spirit is called the Spirit of Christ. The Spirit of Christ in this passage does not mean a Christlike spirit. It means something far more than that—it is a name of the Holy Spirit. Why is the Holy Spirit called the Spirit of Christ? For several reasons.

Because He is Christ's gift.

The Holy Spirit is not merely the gift of the Father, but the gift of the Son as well. We read in John 20:22 that Jesus "breathed on them and saith unto them, Receive ye the Holy Ghost." The Holy Spirit is therefore the breath of Christ as well as the breath of God the Father. It is Christ who breathes upon us and imparts to us the Holy Spirit.

In John 14:15–26, Jesus teaches us that it is in answer to His prayer that the Father gives to us the Holy Spirit. In Acts 2:33 we read that Jesus, "being by the right hand of God exalted, and having received of the Father the promise of the Holy Ghost," shed Him forth upon believers. That verse says that Jesus, having been exalted to the right hand of God in answer to His prayer, receives the Holy Spirit from the Father and sheds forth upon the church Him whom He has received from the Father. In Matthew 3:11 we read that it is Jesus who baptizes with the Holy Spirit. In John 7:37–39 Jesus bids all that are thirsty to come unto Him and drink, and the context makes it clear that the water that He gives is the Holy Spirit who becomes in those who receive Him a source of life and power flowing out to others. It is the glorified Christ who gives to the church the Holy Spirit. In John 4:10, Jesus declares that He is the One who gives the living water, the Holy Spirit. In all these passages, Christ is set forth as the One who gives the Holy Spirit, so the Holy Spirit is called "the Spirit of Christ."

There is a deeper reason why the Holy Spirit is called "the Spirit of Christ"—it is the work of the Holy Spirit to reveal Christ to us.

In John 16:14, we read, "He [the Holy Spirit] shall glorify me: for he shall receive of mine, and shall show it unto you." In a similar way it is written, "But when the Comforter is come, whom I will send unto you from the Father, even the Spirit of truth, which proceedeth from the Father, he shall testify of me." (John 15:26). This is the work of the Holy Spirit to bear witness of Christ and reveal Jesus Christ to men. And as the revealer of Christ, He is called "the Spirit of Christ."

There is a still deeper reason yet why the Holy Spirit is called the Spirit of Christ—it is His work to form Christ as a living presence within us.

In Ephesians 3:16–17, the apostle Paul prays to the Father,

That he would grant you, according to the riches of his glory, to be strengthened with might by his Spirit in the inner man; That Christ may dwell in your hearts by faith.

57

This then is the work of the Holy Spirit, to cause Christ to dwell in our hearts, to form the living Christ within us. Just as the Holy Spirit literally and physically formed Jesus Christ in the womb of the Virgin Mary (see Luke 1:35) so the Holy Spirit spiritually but really forms Jesus Christ within our hearts today. Jesus told His disciples that when the Holy Spirit came that He Himself would come; that is, the result of the coming of the Holy Spirit to dwell in their hearts would be the coming of Christ Himself.

> *And I will pray the Father, and he shall give you another Comforter, that he may abide with you for ever; Even the Spirit of truth; whom the world cannot receive, because it seeth him not, neither knoweth him: but ye know him; for he dwelleth with you, and shall be in you. I will not leave you comfortless: I will come to you.*   *(John 14:16–18)*

It is the privilege of every believer in Christ to have the living Christ formed by the power of the Holy Spirit in his own heart; therefore, the Holy Spirit who thus forms Christ within the heart is called the Spirit of Christ. How wonderful! How glorious is the significance of this name. Let us ponder it until we understand it, as far as it is possible to understand it, and until we rejoice exceedingly in the glory of it.

7. THE SPIRIT OF JESUS CHRIST

The Holy Spirit is called the Spirit of Jesus Christ in Philippians 1:19: "For I know that this shall turn to my salvation through your prayer, and the supply of the Spirit of Jesus Christ." The Spirit is not merely the Spirit of the eternal Word but the Spirit of the Word incarnate; not merely the Spirit of Christ but the Spirit of Jesus Christ. It is the Man Jesus exalted to the right hand of the Father who receives and sends the Spirit. So we read in Acts 2:32–33,

> *This Jesus hath God raised up, whereof we all are witnesses. Therefore being by the right hand of God exalted, and having received of the Father the promise of the Holy Ghost, he hath shed forth this, which ye now see and hear.*

8. THE SPIRIT OF JESUS

The Holy Spirit is called the Spirit of Jesus in Acts 16:6–7 (ASV),

> *And they went through the region of Phrygia and Galatia, having been forbidden of the Holy Spirit to speak the word in Asia; and when they were come over against Mysia, they assayed to go into Bithynia; and the Spirit of Jesus suffered them not.*

By using this name, "The Spirit of Jesus," the thought of the relation of the Spirit to the Man Jesus is still more clear than in the name preceding this, the Spirit of Jesus Christ.

9. THE SPIRIT OF HIS SON

The Holy Spirit is called the Spirit of His Son in Galatians 4:6: "And because ye are sons, God hath sent forth the Spirit of his Son into your hearts, crying, Abba, Father." We see from the context of the preceding verses:

But when the fulness of the time was come, God sent forth his Son, made of a woman, made under the law, To redeem them that were under the law, that we might receive the adoption of sons. (Gal. 4:4–5)

that this name is given to the Holy Spirit in special connection with His testifying to the sonship of the believer. It is "the Spirit of His Son" who testifies to our sonship. The thought is that the Holy Spirit is a filial Spirit, a Spirit who produces a sense of sonship in us. If we receive the Holy Spirit, we no longer think of God as if we were serving under constraint and bondage, but we are sons living in joyous liberty. We do not fear God, we trust Him and rejoice in Him. When we receive the Holy Spirit, we do not receive a "spirit of bondage again to fear" but "the Spirit of adoption, whereby we cry, Abba, Father" (Rom. 8:15). This name of the Holy Spirit is one of the most suggestive of all. We do well to ponder it long until we realize the glad fullness of its significance. We will take it up again when we come to study the work of the Holy Spirit.

10. THE HOLY SPIRIT

This name is of very frequent occurrence, and the name with which most of us are most familiar. One of the most familiar passages in which the name is used is Luke 11:13: "If ye then, being evil, know how to give good gifts unto your children: how much more shall your heavenly Father give the Holy Spirit to them that ask him?" This name emphasizes the essential moral character of the Spirit. He is holy in Himself. We are so familiar with the name that we neglect to weigh its significance. Oh, if we only realized more deeply and constantly that He is the Holy Spirit! We would do well if we, as the seraphim in Isaiah's vision, would bow in His presence and cry, "Holy, holy, holy" (Isa. 6:3). Yet how thoughtlessly we oftentimes talk about Him and pray for Him. We pray for Him to come into our churches and into our hearts but what would He find if He should come there? Would He not find much that would be painful and agonizing to Him?

What would we think if vile women from the lowest den of iniquity in a great city should go to the purest woman in the city and invite her to come and live with them in their disgusting vileness with no intention of changing their evil ways? But that would not be as shocking as for you and me to ask the Holy Spirit to come and dwell in our hearts when we have no intentions of giving up our impurity or our selfishness or our worldliness or our sin. It would not be as shocking as it is for us to invite the Holy Spirit to come into our churches when they are full of worldliness and selfishness and contention and envy and pride and all that is unholy.

However, if the denizens of the lowest and vilest den of infamy should go to the purest and most Christlike woman asking her to go and dwell with them with the intention of putting away everything that was vile and evil and giving to this holy and Christlike woman the entire control of the place, she would go. And as sinful and selfish and imperfect as we may be, the infinitely holy Spirit is ready to come and take His dwelling in our hearts if we will surrender to Him the absolute control of our lives and allow Him to bring everything in thought and fancy and feeling and purpose and imagination and action into conformity with His will. The infinitely holy Spirit is ready to come into our churches, however imperfect and worldly they may be now, if we are willing to put the absolute control of everything in His hands. But let us never forget that He is the Holy Spirit; when we pray for Him, let us pray for Him as such.

11. THE HOLY SPIRIT OF PROMISE

The Holy Spirit is called the Holy Spirit of Promise in Ephesians 1:13: "In whom ye also trusted, after that ye heard the word of truth, the gospel of your salvation: in whom, also after that ye believed, ye were sealed with that holy Spirit of promise." We have here the same name as that given above with the added thought that this Holy

Spirit is the great promise of the Father and of the Son. The Holy Spirit is God's great all-inclusive promise for the present dispensation. The one thing for which Jesus bade the disciples wait after His ascension before they undertook His work was "the promise of the Father" (Acts 1:4), that is the Holy Spirit.

The great promise of the Father until the coming of Christ was the coming atoning Savior and King. When Jesus came and died His atoning death upon the cross of Calvary and arose and ascended to the right hand of the Father, then the second great promise of the Father was the Holy Spirit to take the place of our absent Lord. (See Acts 2:33.)

12. THE SPIRIT OF HOLINESS

The Holy Spirit is called the Spirit of Holiness in Romans 1:4: "And declared to be the Son of God with power, according to the spirit of holiness, by the resurrection from the dead." At the first glance it may seem as if there were no essential difference between the two names, the Holy Spirit and the Spirit of Holiness, but there is a marked difference. The name of the Holy Spirit, as already said, emphasizes the essential moral character of the Spirit as holy, but the name of the Spirit of Holiness brings out the thought that the Holy Spirit is not merely holy in Himself but He imparts holiness to others. The perfect holiness which He Himself possesses He imparts to those who receive Him. (Compare 1 Peter 1:2.)

13. THE SPIRIT OF JUDGMENT

The Holy Spirit is called the Spirit of Judgment in Isaiah 4:4: "When the Lord shall have washed away the filth of the daughters of Zion, and shall have purged the blood of Jerusalem from the midst thereof by the spirit of judgment, and by the spirit of burning." There are two names of the Holy Spirit in this passage. The first is the Spirit of Judgment. The Holy Spirit is so called because it is His work to bring sin to light, to convict of sin. (Compare John 16:7–9.) When the Holy Spirit comes to us, the first thing that He does is to open our eyes to see our sins as God sees them. He judges our sin. (We will go into this more at length in studying John 16:7–11 when considering the work of the Holy Spirit.)

14. THE SPIRIT OF BURNING

This name is used in the passage just quoted above. This name emphasizes His searching, refining, rubbish-consuming, illuminating, and energizing work. The Holy Spirit is like a fire in the heart in which He dwells, and as fire tests and refines and consumes and illuminates and warms and energizes, so does He. In the context, it is the cleansing work of the Holy Spirit which is especially emphasized. (See Isaiah 4:3–4.)

15. THE SPIRIT OF TRUTH

The Holy Spirit is called the Spirit of Truth in John 14:17: "Even the Spirit of truth; whom the world cannot receive, because it seeth him not, neither knoweth him: but ye know him; for he dwelleth with you, and shall be in you." (Compare John 15:26; 16:13.) The Holy Spirit is called the Spirit of Truth because it is the work of the Holy Spirit to communicate and to impart truth to those who receive Him. This comes out in the passage given above, and, if possible, it comes out even more clearly in John 16:13: "Howbeit when he, the Spirit of truth, is come, he will guide you into all truth: for he shall not speak of himself; but whatsoever he shall hear, that shall he speak: and he will show you things to come." All truth is from the Holy Spirit. It is only as He teaches us that we come to know the truth.

16. THE SPIRIT OF WISDOM AND UNDERSTANDING

The Holy Spirit is called the Spirit of Wisdom and Understanding in Isaiah 11:2: "And the spirit of the LORD shall rest upon him, the spirit of wisdom and understanding, the spirit of counsel and might, the spirit of knowledge and of the fear of the LORD." The significance of the name is so plain as to need no explanation. It is evident both from the words used and from the context that it is the work of the Holy Spirit to impart wisdom and understanding to those who receive Him. Those who receive the Holy Spirit receive the Spirit "of power, and of love, and of a sound mind [or sound sense]" (2 Tim. 1:7).

17. THE SPIRIT OF COUNSEL AND MIGHT

We find this name used of the Holy Spirit in the passage given under the preceding section. The meaning of this name is also obvious; the Holy Spirit is called "the spirit of counsel and of might" because He gives us counsel in all our plans and strength to carry them out. (Compare Acts 1:8; 8:29; 16:6–7.) It is our privilege to have God's own counsel in all our plans and God's strength in all the work that we undertake for Him. We receive them by receiving the Holy Spirit, the Spirit of Counsel and Might.

18. THE SPIRIT OF KNOWLEDGE AND OF THE FEAR OF THE LORD

This name also is used in the passage given above (Isa. 11:2). The significance of this name is also obvious. It is the work of the Holy Spirit to impart knowledge to us and to beget in us a reverence for Jehovah, a reverence that reveals itself above all in obedience to His commandments. The one who receives the Holy Spirit finds his delight in the fear of the LORD (Isa. 11:3). The three suggestive names just given refer especially to the gracious work of the Holy Spirit in the servant of the Lord, that is Jesus Christ. (See Isaiah 11:1–5.)

19. THE SPIRIT OF LIFE

The Holy Spirit is called the Spirit of Life in Romans 8:2: "For the law of the Spirit of life in Christ Jesus hath made me free from the law of sin and death." The Holy Spirit is called the Spirit of Life because it is His work to impart life. (Compare John 6:63 RV; Ezekiel 37:1–10.) In the context in which the name is found in the passage given above, beginning back in Romans 7:7, Paul is drawing a contrast between the law of Moses outside a man—holy and just and good, it is true, but impotent—and the living Spirit of God in the heart, imparting spiritual and moral life to the believer and enabling him thus to meet the requirements of the law of God. He draws this contrast to show that what the law alone could not do, in that it was weak through the flesh, the Spirit of God imparting life to the believer and dwelling in the heart enables him to do. Therefore, the righteousness of the law is fulfilled in those who walk not after the flesh but after the Spirit:

> For the law of the Spirit of life in Christ Jesus hath made me free from the law of sin and death. For what the law could not do, in that it was weak through the flesh, God sending his own Son in the likeness of sinful flesh, and for sin, condemned sin in the flesh: That the righteousness of the law might be fulfilled in us, who walk not after the flesh, but after the Spirit.   (Rom. 8:2–4)

The Holy Spirit is therefore called the Spirit of Life, because He imparts spiritual life and consequent victory over sin to those who receive Him.

20. THE OIL OF GLADNESS

The Holy Spirit is called the Oil of Gladness in Hebrews 1:9: "Thou hast loved righteousness, and hated iniquity; therefore God, even thy God, hath anointed thee with the oil of gladness above thy fellows." Someone may ask what reason have we for supposing that "the oil of gladness" in this passage is a name of the Holy Spirit. The answer is found in a comparison of Hebrews 1:9 with Acts 10:38 and Luke 4:18. In Acts 10:38 we read, "How God anointed Jesus of Nazareth with the Holy Ghost and with power," and in Luke 4:18, Jesus Himself is recorded as saying, "The Spirit of the Lord is upon me, because he hath anointed me to preach the gospel to the poor." In both of these passages, we are told it was the Holy Spirit with which Jesus was anointed. As in the passage in Hebrews, we are told that it was with the oil of gladness that He was anointed; therefore, of course, the only possible conclusion is that the oil of gladness means the Holy Spirit. What a beautiful and suggestive name it is for Him whose fruit is, first, "love" and then "joy" (Gal. 5:22).

The Holy Spirit becomes a source of boundless joy to those who receive Him. He so fills and satisfies the soul, that the soul who receives Him "shall never thirst" (John 4:14). No matter how great the afflictions with which the believer receives the Word, still he will have the "joy of the Holy Ghost" (1 Thess. 1:6).

On the Day of Pentecost, when the disciples were baptized with the Holy Spirit, they were so filled with ecstatic joy that others looking on them thought they were intoxicated. They said, "These men are full of new wine" (Acts 2:13). Paul draws a comparison between abnormal intoxication that comes through excess of wine and the wholesome exhilaration from which there is no reaction that comes through being filled with the Spirit:

> *And be not drunk with wine, wherein is excess; but be filled with the Spirit; Speaking to yourselves in psalms and hymns and spiritual songs, singing and making melody in your heart to the Lord; Giving thanks always for all things unto God and the Father in the name of our Lord Jesus Christ.*
>
> *(Eph. 5:18–20)*

When God anoints one with the Holy Spirit, it is as if He broke a precious alabaster box of oil of gladness above their heads until it ran down to the hem of their garments and the whole person was suffused with joy unspeakable and full of glory.

21. THE SPIRIT OF GRACE

The Holy Spirit is called the Spirit of Grace in Hebrews 10:29:

> *Of how much sorer punishment, suppose ye, shall he be thought worthy, who hath trodden under foot the Son of God, and hath counted the blood of the covenant, wherewith he was sanctified, an unholy thing, and hath done despite unto the Spirit of grace?*

This name brings out the fact that it is the Holy Spirit's work to administer and apply the grace of God. He Himself is gracious, it is true, but the name means far more than that. The name means that He makes the manifold grace of God ours experientially. It is only by the work of the Spirit of Grace in our hearts that we are enabled to appropriate to ourselves that infinite fullness of grace that God has bestowed upon us from the beginning in Jesus Christ. It is ours from the beginning, as far as belonging to us is concerned, but it is only ours experientially as we claim it by the power of the Spirit of Grace.

22. THE SPIRIT OF GRACE AND OF SUPPLICATION

The Holy Spirit is called the Spirit of Grace and of Supplication in Zechariah 12:10 (RV):

And I will pour upon the house of David, and upon the inhabitants of Jerusalem, the spirit of grace and of supplication; and they shall look unto me whom they have pierced; and they shall mourn for him, as one mourneth for his only son, and shall be in bitterness for him, as one that is in bitterness for his firstborn.

The phrase, "the spirit of grace and of supplication" in this passage is beyond a doubt a name of the Holy Spirit.

The name "the Spirit of grace" we have already studied in the previous section, but here there is a further thought of that operation of grace that leads us to pray intensely. The Holy Spirit is so called because it is He who teaches us to pray because all true prayer is in the Spirit: "But ye, beloved, building up yourselves on your most holy faith, praying in the Holy Ghost" (Jude 1:20). We of ourselves know not how to pray as we ought, but it is the work of the Holy Spirit of intercession to make "intercession for us with groanings which cannot be uttered" and to lead us out in prayer "according to the will of God" (Rom. 8:26–27). The secret of all true and effective praying is knowing the Holy Spirit as the Spirit of Grace and of Supplication.

23. THE SPIRIT OF GLORY

The Holy Spirit is called the Spirit of Glory in 1 Peter 4:14: "If ye be reproached for the name of Christ, happy are ye; for the spirit of glory and of God resteth upon you: on their part he is evil spoken of, but on your part he is glorified." This name does not merely teach that the Holy Spirit is infinitely glorious Himself, but rather it teaches that He imparts the glory of God to us, just as the Spirit of Truth imparts truth to us. As the Spirit of Life imparts life to us; as the Spirit of Wisdom and Understanding and of Counsel and Might and Knowledge and of the Fear of the LORD imparts to us wisdom and understanding and counsel and might and knowledge and the fear of the LORD; and as the Spirit of Grace applies and administers to us the manifold grace of God; so the Spirit of Glory is the administrator to us of God's glory.

In the immediately preceding verse we read, "But rejoice, inasmuch as ye are partakers of Christ's sufferings; that, when his glory shall be revealed, ye may be glad also with exceeding joy"

(1 Pet. 4:13). It is in this connection that He is called the Spirit of Glory. We find a similar connection between the sufferings which we endure and the glory which the Holy Spirit imparts to us:

> *The Spirit itself beareth witness with our spirit, that we are children of God: And if children, then heirs; heirs of God, and joint-heirs with Christ; if so be that we suffer with him, that we may be also glorified together.*
>   *(Romans 8:16–17)*

The Holy Spirit is the administrator of glory as well as of grace, or rather of the grace that culminates in glory.

24. THE ETERNAL SPIRIT

The Holy Spirit is called the Eternal Spirit in Hebrews 9:14: "How much more shall the blood of Christ, who through the eternal Spirit offered himself without spot to God, purge your conscience from dead works to serve the living God?" The eternity and the deity and infinite majesty of the Holy Spirit are brought out by this name.

25. THE COMFORTER

The Holy Spirit is called the Comforter over and over again in the Scriptures. For example in John 14:26, we read, "But the Comforter which is the Holy Ghost, whom the Father will send in my name, he shall teach you all things, and bring all things to your remembrance, whatsoever I have said unto you." And in John 15:26: "But when the Comforter is come, whom I will send unto you from the Father, even the Spirit of truth, which proceedeth from the Father, he shall testify of me." (See also John 16:27.)

The word translated "Comforter" in these passages means that, but it means much more besides. It is a word difficult of adequate translation into any one word in English. The translators of the Revised Version found difficulty in deciding with what word to render the Greek word so translated. They have suggested in the margin of the Revised Version "Advocate" or "Helper" and a simple transference of the Greek word into English, "Paraclete."

The word translated "Comforter" means literally, "one called to another's side," the idea being, one right at hand to take another's part. It is the same word that is translated "advocate" in 1 John 2:1: "My little children, these things write I unto you, that ye sin not. And if any man sin, we have an advocate with the Father, Jesus Christ the righteous." The word *advocate*, as we now understand it, does not give the full force of the Greek word so rendered. Etymologically, *advocate* means nearly the same thing. *Advocate* is from the Latin, "advocatus," and means "one called to another to take his part," but in our modern usage, the word has acquired a restricted meaning. The Greek word, *Parakletos*, is translated "Comforter" and means "one called alongside," that is, one called to stand constantly by one's side and who is ever ready to stand by us and take our part in everything in which his help is needed. It is a wonderfully tender and expressive name for the Holy One. Sometimes when we think of the Holy Spirit, He seems to be so far away, but when we think of the *Parakletos*, or in plain English our "Standbyer" or our "Part-taker," how near He is.

Up to the time that Jesus made this promise to the disciples, He Himself had been their *Parakletos*. When they were in any emergency or difficulty they turned to Him. On one occasion, for example, the disciples were in doubt as to how to pray, and they turned to Jesus and said, "Lord, teach us to pray" (Luke 11:1). And the Lord taught them this wonderful prayer that has come down through the ages:

> *And he said unto them, When ye pray, say, Our Father which art in heaven, Hallowed be thy name. Thy kingdom come. Thy will be done, as in heaven, so in earth. Give us day by day our daily bread. And forgive us our sins; for we also forgive every one that is indebted to us. And lead us not into temptation; but deliver us from evil.   (Luke 11:2–4)*

On another occasion, Peter was sinking in the waves of Galilee and cried, "Lord, save me" (Matt. 14:30), and "immediately Jesus stretched forth his hand, and caught him" (Matt. 14:31) and saved him. In every extremity they turned to Him. Likewise, now that Jesus is gone to the Father, we have another person, just as divine as He is, just as wise as He, just as strong as He, just as loving as

He, just as tender as He, just as ready, and just as able to help, who is always right by our side. Yes, better yet, He dwells in our hearts and will take hold and help if we only trust Him to do it.

If the truth of the Holy Spirit as set forth in the name *Parakletos* once gets into our heart and abides there, it will banish all loneliness forever, for how can we ever be lonely when this best of all friends is ever with us? In the last eight years, I have been called upon to endure what would naturally be a very lonely life. Most of the time I am separated from my wife and children by the calls of duty. For eighteen months consecutively, I was separated from almost all my family by many thousands of miles. The loneliness would have been unendurable were it not for the one all-sufficient Friend, who was always with me.

I recall one night walking up and down the deck of a storm-tossed steamer in the South Seas. Most of my family were eighteen thousand miles away; the remaining member of my family was not with me. The officers were busy on the bridge. I was pacing the deck alone, and the thought came to me, "Here you are all alone." Then another thought came, "I am not alone; by my side as I walk this deck in the loneliness and the storm walks the Holy Spirit," and He was enough. I said something like this once at a Bible conference in St. Paul. A doctor came to me at the close of the meeting and gently said, "I want to thank you for that thought about the Holy Spirit always being with us. I am a doctor. Often I have to drive far out in the country in the night and storm to attend a case, and I have often been so lonely, but I will never be lonely again. I will always know that by my side in my doctor's carriage, the Holy Spirit goes with me."

If this thought of the Holy Spirit as the ever-present Paraclete once gets into your heart and abides there, it will banish all fear forever. How can we be afraid in the face of any peril, if this divine One is by our side to counsel us and to take our part? There may be a howling mob about us or a lowering storm; it does not matter. He stands between us and both mob and storm.

One night I had promised to walk four miles to a friend's house after an evening session of a conference. The path led along the side of a lake. As I started for my friend's house, a thunderstorm was coming up. I had not counted on this, but as I had promised, I felt I ought to go. The path led along the edge of the lake, oftentimes very near to the edge. Sometimes the lake was near the path and sometimes many feet below. The night was so dark with the clouds, I could not see ahead. Now and then there would be a blinding flash of lightning in which I could see where the path was washed away, and then it would be blacker than ever. I could hear the lake booming below. It seemed a dangerous place to walk. But that very week I had been speaking upon the personality of the Holy Spirit and about the Holy Spirit as an ever-present friend, and the thought came to me, "What was it you were telling the people in the address about the Holy Spirit as an ever-present friend?" And then I said to myself, "Between me and the boiling lake and the edge of the path walks the Holy Spirit," and I pushed on, fearless and glad.

When we were in London, a young lady attended the meeting one afternoon in the Royal Albert Hall. She had an abnormal fear of the dark. It was absolutely impossible for her to go into a dark room alone, but the thought of the Holy Spirit as an ever-present Friend sank into her mind. She went home and told her mother what a wonderful thought she had heard that day and how it had banished forever all fear from her. It was already growing very dark in the London winter afternoon, and her mother looked up and said, "Very well, let us see if it is real. Go up to the top of the house and shut yourself alone in a dark room." She instantly sprang to her feet, bounded up the stairs, went into a room that was totally dark, shut the door, and sat down. All fear was gone, and as she wrote the next day, the whole room seemed to be filled with a wonderful glory, the glory of the presence of the Holy Spirit.

In the thought of the Holy Spirit as the Paraclete there is also a cure for insomnia. For two awful years, I suffered from insomnia. Night after night I would go to bed apparently almost dead from lack of sleep. It seemed as though I must sleep, but I could not sleep. Oh, the agony of those two years! It seemed as if I would lose my mind if I did not get relief. Relief came at last, and for years I went on without the suggestion of trouble from insomnia. Then one night I retired to my room in the institute and lay down expecting to fall asleep in a moment as I usually did. But scarcely had my head touched the pillow when I became aware that insomnia was back again. If one has ever had it, he never forgets it and never mistakes it. It seemed as if insomnia were sitting on the foot board of my bed, grinning at me and saying, "I am back again for another two years." "Oh," I thought, "two more awful years of insomnia."

However, that very morning, I had been lecturing to our students in the institute about the personality of the Holy Spirit and about the Holy Spirit as an ever-present friend. At once the thought came to me, "What were you talking to the students about this morning? What were you telling them?" And, I looked up and said, "Blessed Spirit of God, You are here. I am not alone. If You have anything to say to me, I will listen," and He began to open to me some of the deep and precious things about my Lord and Savior, things that filled my soul with joy and rest. The next thing I knew I was asleep, and the next thing I knew it was the following morning. So, whenever insomnia has come my way since, I have simply remembered that the Holy Spirit was there, and I have looked up to Him to speak to me and to teach me. He has done so, and insomnia has taken its flight.

In the thought of the Holy Spirit as the Paraclete, there is a cure for a breaking heart. How many aching, breaking hearts there are in this world of ours, so full of death and separation from those we most dearly love. Example after example could be given of a women who, a few months or a few weeks ago, had no care or no worry, for by her side was a Christian husband who was so wise and strong that the wife rested all responsibility upon him and walked carefree through life and was satisfied with his love and companionship. But one awful day, he was taken from her. She was left alone, and all the cares and responsibilities rested upon her. How empty that heart has been ever since; how empty the whole world has been. She has just dragged through her life and her duties as best she could with an aching and almost breaking heart. There is One, if she only knew it, wiser and more loving than the tenderest husband, One willing to bear all the care and responsibilities of life for her, One who is able, if she will only let Him, to fill every nook and corner of her empty and aching heart. That One is the Paraclete.

I said something like this in St. Andrews' Hall in Glasgow. At the close of the meeting a sad-faced Christian woman wearing a widow's garb came to me as I stepped out of the hall into the reception room. She hurried to me and said, "Dr. Torrey, this is the anniversary of my dear husband's death. Just one year ago today he was taken from me. I came today to see if you could not speak some word to help me. You have given me just the word I need. I will never be lonesome again." A year and a half passed by. I was on the yacht of a friend on the lochs of the Clyde. One day a little boat put out from shore and came alongside the yacht. One of the first to come up the side of the yacht was this widow. She hurried to me, and the first thing she said was, "The thought that you gave me that day in St. Andrews' Hall on the anniversary of my husband's leaving me has been with me ever since, and the Holy Spirit does satisfy me and fill my heart."

It is in our work for our Master that the thought of the Holy Spirit as the Paraclete comes with greatest helpfulness. I think it may be permissible to illustrate it from my own experience. I entered the ministry because I was literally forced to. For years I refused to become a Christian because I was determined that I would not be a preacher, and I feared that if I surrendered to Christ I must enter the ministry. My conversion turned upon my yielding to Him at this point. The night I yielded, I did not say, "I will accept Christ" or "I will give up sin," or anything of that sort, I simply cried, "Take this awful burden off my heart, and I will preach the Gospel." But no one could be less fitted by natural temperament for the ministry than I.

From early boyhood, I was extraordinarily timid and bashful. Even after I had entered Yale College, when I would go home in the summer and my mother would call me in to meet her friends, I was so frightened that when I thought I spoke I did not make an audible sound. When her friends had gone, my mother would ask, "Why didn't you say something to them?" I would reply that I supposed I had, but my mother would say, "You did not utter a sound." Think of a young fellow like that entering the ministry. I never mustered courage even to speak in a public prayer meeting until after I was in the theological seminary. Then I felt, if I were to enter the ministry, I must be able to at least speak in a prayer meeting. I learned a little piece by heart to say, but when the hour came, I forgot much of it in my terror. At the critical moment, I grasped the back of the settee in front of me and pulled myself hurriedly to my feet and held on to the settee. One Niagara seemed to be going up one side and another down another; my voice faltered. I repeated as much as I could remember and sat down. Think of a man like that entering the ministry. ·

In the early days of my ministry, I would write my sermons out in full and commit them to memory, stand up and twist a button until I had repeated it as best I could, and then sink back into the pulpit chair with a sense of relief that that was over for another week. I cannot tell you what I suffered in those early days of my ministry. But the glad day came when I came to know the Holy Spirit as the Paraclete. The thought got possession of me that when I stood up to preach there was Another who stood by my side. While the audience saw me, God saw Him. The responsibility was all upon Him. He was abundantly able to meet it and care for it all. All I had to do was to stand back as far out of sight as possible and let Him do the work.

I have no dread of preaching now. Preaching is the greatest joy of my life. Sometimes when I stand up to speak and realize that He is there, that all the responsibility is upon Him, such a joy fills my heart that I can scarcely restrain myself from shouting and leaping. He is just as ready to help us in all our work, in our Sunday school classes, in our personal work, and in every other line of Christian effort.

Many hesitate to speak to others about accepting Christ. They are afraid they will not say the right thing; they fear that they will do more harm than they will good. You certainly will if you do it, but if you will just believe in the Paraclete and trust Him to say it and to say it in His way, you will never do harm but always good. It may seem at the time that you have accomplished nothing, but perhaps years later you will find out you have accomplished much. Even if you do not find it out in this world, you will find it out in eternity.

There are many ways in which the Paraclete stands by us and helps us which we will examine at length when we come to study His work. He stands by us when we pray (Rom. 8:26–27); when we study the Word (John 14:26; 16:12–14); when we do personal work (Acts 8:29); when we preach or teach (1 Cor. 2:4); when we are tempted (Rom. 8:2); and when we leave this world (Acts 7:54–60). Let us get this thought firmly fixed now and for all time that the Holy Spirit is One called to our side to take our part.

> Ever present, truest Friend,
> Ever near, Thine aid to lend.

Chapter 6

The Work of the Holy Spirit in the Material Universe

There are many who think of the work of the Holy Spirit as limited to man, but God reveals to us in His Word that the Holy Spirit's work has a far wider scope than this. We are taught in the Bible that the Holy Spirit has a threefold work in the material universe.

The creation of the material universe and of man is effected through the agency of the Holy Spirit.

We read in Psalm 33:6, "By the word of the LORD were the heavens made; and all the host of them by the breath of his mouth." We have already seen in our study of the names of the Holy Spirit that the Holy Spirit is the breath of Jehovah, so this passage teaches us that all the hosts of heaven, all the stellar worlds, were made by the Holy Spirit. We are taught explicitly in Job 33:4 that the creation of man is the Holy Spirit's work. We read, "The spirit of God hath made me, and the breath of the Almighty hath given me life."

Here both the creation of the material frame and the impartation of life are attributed to the agency of the Holy Spirit.

In other passages of Scripture we are taught that creation was in and through the Son of God. For example we read in Colossians 1:16, "For by him were all things created, that are in heaven and that are in earth, visible and invisible, whether they be thrones, or dominions, or principalities, or powers: all things were created by him and for him." In a similar way we read in Hebrews 1:2, that God "hath in these last days spoken unto us by his Son, whom He appointed heir of all things, *through whom* also He made the worlds [ages]." In the passage given above (Ps. 33:6), the Word as well as the Spirit are mentioned in connection with creation. In the account of the creation and the rehabilitation of this world to be the abode of man, Father, Word, and Holy Spirit are all mentioned. (See Genesis 1:1–3.) It is evident from a comparison of these passages that the Father, Son, and Holy Spirit are all active in the creative work. The Father works in His Son, through His Spirit.

The maintenance of living creatures is attributed to the agency of the Holy Spirit in the Bible.

The original creation of the material universe is not the only matter attributed to the agency of the Holy Spirit as we can see in the following verses:

Thou hidest thy face, they are troubled: thou takest away their breath, they die, and

return to their dust. Thou sendes
spirit, they are created: and thou
the face of the earth.   (Psalm 10

The clear indication of this passage is th   ...ny
are things brought into being through the agency
of the Holy Spirit but that they are maintained in
being by the Holy Spirit. Not only is spiritual life
maintained by the Spirit of God but material being
as well. Things exist and continue by the presence
of the Spirit of God in them. This does not mean
for a moment that the universe is God, but it does
mean that the universe is maintained in its being
by the immanence of God in it. This is the great
and solemn truth that lies at the foundation of the
awful and debasing perversions of pantheism in its
countless forms.

The development of the material universe into higher states of order is attributed to the agency of the Holy Spirit.

Not only is the universe created through the
agency of the Holy Spirit and maintained in its
existence through the agency of the Holy Spirit,
but the development of the earlier, chaotic, unde-
veloped states of the material universe into higher
orders of being is effected through the working of
the Holy Spirit. We read in Genesis,

And the earth was [or became] *without
form, and void; and darkness was upon the
face of the deep. And the Spirit of God*

85

*ed upon the face of the waters. And God
said, Let there be light: and there was light.*
(Gen. 1:2–3)

We may take this account to refer either to the
original creation of the universe, or we may take it
as the deeper students of the Word are more and
more inclining to take it, as the account of the rehabilitation of the earth after its plunging into
chaos through sin after the original creation described in verse one. In either case we have set before us here the development of the earth from a
chaotic and unformed condition into its present
highly developed condition through the agency of
the Holy Spirit.

We see the process carried still further in
Genesis 2:7: "And the LORD God formed man of
the dust of the ground, and breathed into his nostrils the breath of life; and man became a living
soul." Here again it is through the agency of the
breath of God that a higher thing, human life,
comes into being. Naturally, as the Bible is the
history of man's redemption it does not dwell upon
this phase of truth, but seemingly each new and
higher impartation of the Spirit of God brings
forth a higher order of being: first, inert matter;
then motion; then light; then vegetable life; then
animal life; then man; and, as we shall see later,
then the new man; and then Jesus Christ, the supreme Man, the completion of God's thought of
man, the Son of Man. This is the biblical thought
of development from the lower to the higher by the
agency of the Spirit of God as distinguished from

the godless evolution that has been so popular in the present generation. It is, however, only hinted at in the Bible. The more important phases of the Holy Spirit's work, His work in redemption, are those that are emphasized and stated and reiterated. The Word of God is even more plainly active in each state of progress of creation. "God said" occurs ten times in the first chapter of Genesis.

Chapter 7

The Holy Spirit Convicts the World

Our salvation begins experientially with our being brought to a profound sense that we need a Savior. The Holy Spirit is the One who brings us to this realization of our need. We read in John 16:8–11 (ASV),

> And he, when he is come, will convict the world in respect of sin, and of righteousness, and of judgment: of sin, because they believe not on me; of righteousness, because I go to the Father, and ye behold me no more; of judgment, because the prince of this world hath been judged.

We see in this passage that it is the work of the Holy Spirit to convict men of sin.

That is, to so convince men of their error in respect to sin as to produce a deep sense of personal guilt. We have the first recorded fulfillment of this promise in Acts:

> Therefore let all the house of Israel know assuredly, that God hath made that same

Jesus, whom ye have crucified, both Lord and Christ. Now when they heard this, they were pricked in their heart, and said unto Peter and to the rest of the apostles, Men and brethren, what shall we do? (Acts 2:36–37)

The Holy Spirit had come just as Jesus had promised that He would, and when He came, He convicted the world of sin. He pricked them in their hearts with a sense of their awful guilt in the rejection of their Lord and their Christ. If the apostle Peter had spoken the same words the day before Pentecost, no such results would have followed. But now Peter was filled with the Holy Spirit (see Acts 2:4), and the Holy Spirit took Peter and his words and, through the instrumentality of Peter and his words, convicted his hearers. The Holy Spirit is the only One who can convince men of sin.

"The [natural] heart is deceitful above all things, and desperately wicked" (Jer. 17:9), and there is nothing in which the inbred deceitfulness of our hearts comes out more clearly than in our estimations of ourselves. We are all of us sharp-sighted enough to the faults of others, but we are all blind by nature to our own faults. Our blindness to our own shortcomings is oftentimes little short of ludicrous. We have a strange power of exaggerating our imaginary virtues and utterly losing sight of our defects. The longer and more thoroughly one studies human nature, the more clearly he will see how hopeless the task is of convincing other men of sin. We cannot do it, nor has

God left it for us to do. He has put this work into the hands of One who is abundantly able to do it—the Holy Spirit.

One of the worst mistakes that we can make in our efforts to bring men to Christ is to try to convince them of sin in any power of our own. Unfortunately, it is one of the commonest mistakes. Preachers will stand in the pulpit and argue and reason with men to make them see and realize that they are sinners. They make it as plain as day. It is a wonder that their hearers do not see it, but they do not. Personal workers sit down beside an inquirer and reason with him and bring forward passages of Scripture in a most skillful way—the very passages that are calculated to produce the desired effect—and yet there is no result. Why? Because we are trying to do the Holy Spirit's work—the work that He alone can do—to convince men of sin. If we would only bear in mind our own utter inability to convince men of sin and cast ourselves upon Him in utter helplessness to do the work, we would see results.

At the close of an inquiry meeting in our church in Chicago, one of our best workers brought to me an engineer on the Pan Handle Railway with the remark, "I wish that you would speak to this man. I have been talking to him two hours with no result." I sat down by his side with my open Bible, and in less than ten minutes that man, under deep conviction of sin, was on his knees crying to God for mercy.

The worker who had brought him to me said when the man had gone out, "That is very strange."

"What is strange?" I asked.

"Do you know," the worker said, "I used exactly the same passages in dealing with that man that you did, and though I had worked with him for two hours with no result, in ten minutes with the same passages of Scripture, he was brought under conviction of sin and accepted Christ."

What was the explanation? Simply this, for once that worker had forgotten something that she seldom forgot, namely, that the Holy Spirit must do the work. She had been trying to convince the man of sin. She had used the right passages; she had reasoned wisely; she had made out a clear case; but she had not looked to the only One who could do the work. When she brought the man to me and said, "I have worked with him for two hours with no result," I thought to myself, "If this expert worker has dealt with him for two hours with no result, what is the use of my dealing with him?" In a sense of utter helplessness, I cast myself upon the Holy Spirit to do the work, and He did it.

While we cannot convince men of sin, there is One who can, the Holy Spirit. He can convince the most hardened and blinded man of sin. He can change men and women from utter carelessness and indifference to a place where they are overwhelmed with a sense of their need of a Savior. How often we have seen this illustrated.

Some years ago, the officers of the Chicago Avenue Church were burdened with the fact that there was so little profound conviction of sin manifested in our meetings. There were conversions, a good many were being added to the church, but very few were coming with an apparently overwhelming conviction of sin. One night one of the officers of the church said, "Fellow believers, I am greatly troubled by the fact that we have so little conviction of sin in our meetings. While we are having conversions and many accessions to the church, there is not that deep conviction of sin that I like to see. I propose that we, the officers of the church, meet from night to night to pray that there may be more conviction of sin in our meetings." The suggestion was taken up by the entire committee.

We had not been praying many nights when one Sunday evening I saw in the front seat underneath the gallery a showily dressed man with a very hard face. A large diamond was blazing from his shirt front. He was sitting beside one of the deacons. As I looked at him as I preached, I thought to myself, "That man is a gambling man, and Deacon Young has been fishing today." It turned out that I was right. The man was the son of a woman who kept a gambling house in a Western city. I think he had never been in a Protestant service before. Deacon Young had gotten hold of him that day on the street and had brought him to the meeting. As I preached, the man's eyes were riveted upon me. When we went downstairs to the after-meeting, Deacon Young took the man with him. I was late dealing with the anxious that night. As I finished with the last one about eleven o'clock and almost everybody had gone home, Deacon Young came over to me and said, "I have a man over here I wish you would come and speak with." It was this big gambler. He was deeply agitated.

"Oh," he groaned, "I don't know what is the matter with me. I never felt this way before in all my life," and he sobbed and shook like a leaf. Then he told me this story: "I started out this afternoon to go down to Cottage Grove Avenue to meet some men and spend the afternoon gambling. As I passed by the park over yonder, some of your young men were holding an open air meeting, and I stopped to listen. I saw one man testifying whom I had known in a life of sin, and I waited to hear what he had to say. When he finished, I went on down the street. I had not gone far when some strange power took hold of me and brought me back, and I stayed through the meeting. Then this gentleman spoke to me and brought me over to your church, to your Yoke Fellows' Meeting. I stayed for supper with them, and he brought me up to hear you preach. Then he brought me down to this meeting." Here he stopped and sobbed, "Oh, I don't know what is the matter with me. I feel awful. I never felt this way before in all my life," and his great frame shook with emotion.

"I know what is the matter with you," I said. "You are under conviction of sin; the Holy Spirit is dealing with you," and I pointed him to Christ. He knelt down and cried to God for mercy, to forgive his sins for Christ's sake.

Not long after, one Sunday night I saw another man sitting in the gallery almost exactly above where this man had sat. A diamond flashed also from this man's shirt front. I said to myself, "There is another gambling man." He turned out to be a traveling man who was also a gambler. As I preached, he leaned further and further forward in his seat. In the midst of my sermon, without any intention of giving out the invitation, simply wishing to drive a point home, I said, "Who will accept Jesus Christ tonight?" Quick as a flash the man sprang to his feet and shouted, "I will." It rang through the building like the crack of a revolver. I dropped my sermon and instantly gave out the invitation; men and women and young people rose all over the building to yield themselves to Christ. God was answering prayer, and the Holy Spirit was convincing men of sin.

The Holy Spirit can convince men of sin. We need not despair of anyone, no matter how indifferent they may appear, no matter how worldly, no matter how self-satisfied, no matter how irreligious. The Holy Spirit can convince men of sin.

A young minister of very rare culture and ability once came to me and said, "I have a great problem on my hands. I am the pastor of the church in a university town. My congregation is largely made up of university professors and students. They are most delightful people. They have very high moral ideals and are living most exemplary lives. Now," he continued, "if I had a congregation in which there were drunkards and outcasts and thieves, I could convince them of sin, but my problem is how to make people like that, the most delightful people in the world, believe that they are sinners—how to convict them of sin."

I replied, "It is impossible. You cannot do it, but the Holy Spirit can." And so He can. Some of the deepest manifestations of conviction of sin I have ever seen have been on the part of men and women of most exemplary conduct and attractive personality. But they were sinners, and the Holy Spirit opened their eyes to the fact.

While it is the Holy Spirit who convinces men of sin, He does it through us. This comes out very clearly in the context of the passage before us (John 16:8–11). Jesus says in the preceding verse, "Nevertheless I tell you the truth; It is expedient for you that I go away: for if I go not away, the Comforter will not come unto you; but if I depart, I will send him unto you" (John 16:7). Then He goes on to say, "And he, when he is come [unto you], will convict the world in respect of sin" (John 16:8 ASV). That is, our Lord Jesus sends the Holy Spirit to us (to believers), and when He is come to us believers, through us to whom He has come, He convinces the world. On the Day of Pentecost, it was the Holy Spirit who convinced the three thousand of sin, but the Holy Spirit came to the group of believers and through them convinced the outside world.

As far as the Holy Scriptures definitely tell us, the Holy Spirit has no way of getting at the unsaved world except through the agency of those who are already saved. Every conversion recorded in the Acts of the Apostles was through the agency of men or women already saved. Take, for example, the conversion of Saul of Tarsus. If there ever were a miraculous conversion, it was that.

The glorified Jesus appeared visibly to Saul on his way to Damascus, but before Saul could come out clearly into the light as a saved man, human instrumentality had to be brought in. Prostrate on the ground, Saul cried to the risen Christ asking what he must do, and the Lord told him to go into Damascus and there it would be told him what he must do. And then Ananias, "a certain disciple" (Acts 9:10), was brought on the scene as the human instrumentality through whom the Holy Spirit could do His work. (See Acts 9:17; 22:16.)

Take the case of Cornelius. Here again was a most remarkable conversion through supernatural agency. An angel appeared to Cornelius, but the angel did not tell Cornelius what to do to be saved. The angel rather said to Cornelius, "Send men to Joppa, and call for Simon, whose surname is Peter; who shall tell thee words, whereby thou and all thy house shall be saved" (Acts 11:13–14). So we may go right through the record of the conversions in the Acts of the Apostles, and we will see they were all effected through human instrumentality.

How solemn, how almost overwhelming, is the thought that the Holy Spirit has no way of getting at the unsaved with His saving power except through the instrumentality of those of us who are already Christians. If we realized that, would we not be more careful to offer to the Holy Spirit a more free and unobstructed channel for His all-important work? The Holy Spirit needs human lips to speak through. He needs yours, and He needs lives so clean and so utterly surrendered to Him that He can work through them.

Notice of which sin it is that the Holy Spirit convinces men—the sin of unbelief in Jesus Christ. "Of sin because they believe not on me" (John 16:9), says Jesus. Not the sin of stealing, not the sin of drunkenness, not the sin of adultery, not the sin of murder, but the sin of unbelief in Jesus Christ. The one thing that the eternal God demands of men is that they believe on Him whom He has sent (John 6:29). The one sin that reveals man's rebellion against God and daring defiance of Him is the sin of not believing in Jesus Christ, and this is the one sin that the Holy Spirit puts to the front and emphasizes and of which He convicts men. This was the sin of which He convicted the three thousand on the Day of Pentecost. Doubtless, there were many other sins in their lives, but the one point that the Holy Spirit brought to the front through the apostle Peter was that the One whom they had rejected was their Lord and Christ, attested so to be by His resurrection from the dead. (See Acts 2:22–36.) "Now when they heard this [namely, that He whom they had rejected was Lord and Christ] they were pricked in their heart" (Acts 2:37). This is the sin of which the Holy Spirit convinces men today.

In regard to the comparatively minor moralities of life, there is a wide difference among men, but the thief who rejects Christ and the honest man who rejects Christ are alike condemned at the great point of what they do with God's Son, and this is the point that the Holy Spirit presses home. The sin of unbelief is the most difficult of all sins of which to convince men. The average unbeliever does not look upon unbelief as a sin. Many an unbeliever looks upon his unbelief as a mark of intellectual superiority. Not infrequently, he is all the more proud of it because it is the only mark of intellectual superiority that he possesses. He tosses his head and says, "I am an agnostic," "I am a skeptic," or "I am an infidel," and assumes an air of superiority on that account. If he does not go so far as that, the unbeliever frequently looks upon his unbelief as, at the very worst, a misfortune. He looks for pity rather than for blame. He says, "Oh, I wish I could believe. I am so sorry I cannot believe," and then appeals to us for pity because he cannot believe. But when the Holy Spirit touches a man's heart, he no longer looks upon unbelief as a mark of intellectual superiority. He does not look upon unbelief as a mere misfortune. He sees it as the most daring, decisive, and damning of all sins and is overwhelmed with a sense of his awful guilt in that he had not believed on the name of the only begotten Son of God.

The Holy Spirit not only convicts of sin, He convicts in respect to righteousness.

He convicts the world of righteousness because Jesus Christ has gone to the Father. That is, He convicts (convinces with a convincing that is self-condemning) the world of Christ's righteousness which is attested to by His going to the Father. The coming of the Spirit is in itself a proof that Christ has gone to the Father (see Acts 2:33), and the Holy Spirit thus opens our eyes to see that

Jesus Christ, whom the world condemned as an evil-doer, was indeed the righteous One. The Father sets the stamp of His approval upon His character and claims by raising Him from the dead, exalting Him to His own right hand, and giving to Him a name that is above every name.

The world at large today claims to believe in the righteousness of Christ, but it does not really believe in the righteousness of Christ. It has no adequate conception of the righteousness of Christ. The righteousness which the world attributes to Christ is not the righteousness which God attributes to Him but a poor human righteousness, perhaps a little better than our own. The world loves to put the names of other men that it considers good alongside the name of Jesus Christ. But when the Spirit of God comes to a man, He convinces him of the righteousness of Christ. He opens his eyes to see Jesus Christ standing absolutely alone, not only far above all men but "Far above all principality, and power, and might, and dominion, and every name that is named, not only in this world, but also in that which is to come" (Eph. 1:21).

The Holy Spirit also convicts the world of judgment.

The ground upon which the Holy Spirit convinces men of judgment is upon the ground of the fact that "the prince of this world is judged" (John 16:11). When Jesus Christ was nailed to the cross, it seemed as if He were judged there, but in reality it was the prince of this world who was judged at the cross. By raising Jesus Christ from the dead, the Father made it plain to all coming ages that the cross was not the judgment of Christ but the judgment of the prince of darkness. The Holy Spirit opens our eyes to see this fact and so convinces us of judgment.

There is a great need today that the world be convinced of judgment. Judgment is a doctrine that has fallen into the background, that has indeed almost sunken out of sight. It is not popular today to speak about judgment, retribution, or hell. One who emphasizes judgment and future retribution is not thought to be quite up-to-date; he is considered medieval or even archaic. But when the Holy Spirit opens the eyes of men, they believe in judgment.

In the early days of my Christian experience, I had great difficulties with the Bible doctrine of future retribution. I came again and again up to what it taught about the eternal penalties of persistent sin. It seemed as if I could not believe it: it must not be true. Time and again I would back away from the stern teachings of Jesus Christ and the apostles concerning this matter. But one night I was waiting upon God that I might know the Holy Spirit in a fuller manifestation of His presence and His power. God gave me what I sought that night. With this larger experience of the Holy Spirit's presence and power, there came such a revelation of the glory, the infinite glory of Jesus Christ, that I no longer had any difficulties with what the Book said about the stern and endless judgment that would be visited upon those who persistently rejected this glorious Son of God. From that day to this, while I have had many a heartache over the Bible doctrine of future retribution, I have had no intellectual difficulty with it. I have believed it. The Holy Spirit has convinced me of judgment.

Chapter 8

The Holy Spirit Bearing Witness to Jesus Christ

When our Lord was talking to His disciples on the night before His crucifixion about the Comforter who, after His departure, was to come to take His place, He said,

> But when the Comforter is come, whom I will send unto you from the Father, even the Spirit of truth, which proceedeth from the Father, he shall bear witness of me: and ye also bear witness, because ye have been with me from the beginning. (John 15:26–27 RV)

The apostle Peter and the other disciples, when they were strictly commanded by the Jewish Council not to teach in the name of Jesus, said, "We are his witnesses of these things, and so is also the Holy Ghost" (Acts 5:32). It is clear from these words of Jesus Christ and the apostles that it is the work of the Holy Spirit to bear witness concerning Jesus Christ.

We find the Holy Spirit's testimony to Jesus Christ in the Scriptures, but besides this the Holy

Spirit bears witness directly to the individual heart concerning Jesus Christ. He takes His own Scriptures, interprets them to us, and makes them clear to us. All truth is from the Spirit, for He is "the Spirit of truth" (John 15:26), but it is especially His work to bear witness to Him who is the truth, that is Jesus Christ. (See John 14:6.) It is only through the testimony of the Holy Spirit directly to our hearts that we ever come to a true, living knowledge of Jesus Christ. (Compare 1 Corinthians 12:3.) No amount of mere reading the written Word (in the Bible) and no amount of listening to man's testimony will ever bring us to a living knowledge of Christ. It is only when the Holy Spirit Himself takes the written Word, or takes the testimony of our fellowman, and interprets it directly to our hearts that we really come to see and know Jesus as He is.

On the day of Pentecost, Peter gave all his hearers the testimony of the Scriptures regarding Christ and also gave them his own testimony. He told them what he and the other apostles knew by personal observation regarding His resurrection. Unless the Holy Spirit Himself had taken the Scriptures which Peter had brought together and taken the testimony of Peter and the other disciples, the three thousand would not on that day have seen Jesus as He really was and received Him and been baptized in His name. The Holy Spirit added His testimony to that of Peter and that of the written Word. Mr. Moody used to say in his terse and graphic way that when Peter said, "Therefore let all the house of Israel know assuredly that God hath made that same Jesus, whom ye have crucified, both Lord and Christ" (Acts 2:36), the Holy Spirit said, "Amen," and the people saw and believed. It is certain that unless the Holy Spirit had come that day, and through Peter and the other apostles borne His direct testimony to the hearts of their hearers, there would have been no saving vision of Jesus on the part of the people.

If you wish men to get a true view of Jesus Christ, such a view of Him that they may believe and be saved, it is not enough that you give them the Scriptures concerning Him; it is not enough that you give them your own testimony. You must seek for them the testimony of the Holy Spirit and put yourself into such a relationship with God that the Holy Spirit may bear His testimony through you. Neither your testimony nor that of the written Word alone will effect this even though it is your testimony or that of the Word that the Holy Spirit uses. Unless your testimony and that of the Word is taken up by the Holy Spirit and He Himself testifies, they will not believe.

This explains something which every experienced worker must have noticed. We sit down beside an inquirer and open our Bibles and give him those Scriptures which clearly reveal Jesus as his atoning Savior on the cross, a Savior from the guilt of sin, and as his risen Savior, a Savior from the power of sin. It is just the truth the man needs to see and believe in order to be saved, but he does not see it. We go over these Scriptures which to us are as plain as day again and again, and the inquirer sits there in blank darkness. He sees nothing, he grasps nothing. Sometimes we almost wonder if the inquirer is stupid that he cannot see it. No, he is not stupid, except with that spiritual blindness that possesses every mind unenlightened by the Holy Spirit: "But the natural man receiveth not the things of the Spirit of God: for they are foolishness unto him: neither can he know them, because they are spiritually discerned" (1 Cor. 2:14). We go over it again, and still he does not see it. We go over it again, and his face lightens up as he exclaims, "I see it. I see it." He sees Jesus and believes and is saved and knows he is saved there on the spot. What has happened? Simply this, the Holy Spirit has borne His testimony, and what was dark as midnight before is as clear as day now.

This explains also why it is that one who has been long in darkness concerning Jesus Christ so quickly comes to see the truth when he surrenders his will to God and seeks light from Him. When he surrenders his will to God, he has put himself into that attitude towards God where the Holy Spirit can do His work. (See Acts 5:32.) Jesus says in John 7:17, "If any man will do his [God's] will, he shall know of the doctrine, whether it be of God, or whether I speak of myself." When a man wills to do the will of God, then the conditions are provided on which the Holy Spirit works, and He illuminates the mind to see the truth about Jesus and to see that His teaching is the very Word of God.

John writes in John 20:31, "But these are written [these things in the gospel of John], that ye might believe that Jesus is the Christ, the Son of God; and that believing ye might have life through his name." John wrote his gospel for this purpose: that men might see Jesus as the Christ, the Son of God, through what he recorded and that they might believe that He is the Christ, the Son of God; and that, thus believing, they might have life through His name. The best book in the world to put into the hands of one who desires to know about Jesus and to be saved is the gospel of John. However, many a man has read the gospel of John over and over and over again and has not seen and believed that Jesus is the Christ, the Son of God. But let the same man surrender his will absolutely to God and ask God for light as he reads this gospel and promise God that he will take his stand on everything in the gospel that He shows him to be true, and before the man has finished reading, he will see clearly that Jesus is the Christ, the Son of God, and will believe and have eternal life. Why? Because he has put himself into the place where the Holy Spirit can take the things written in the Gospel and interpret them and bear His testimony. I have seen this tested and proven time and time again all around the world.

Men have come to me and have said to me that they did not believe that Jesus is the Christ, the Son of God, and many have gone farther and said they were agnostics and did not even know whether there was a personal God. Then I have told them to read the gospel of John, that in that gospel John presented the evidence that Jesus was the Christ, the Son of God. Oftentimes, they have told me they have read it repeatedly and yet were not convinced that Jesus was the Christ, the Son of God. Then I have said to them, "You have not read it the right way," and I have urged them to surrender their wills to God (or in the case where they were not sure there was a God, have gotten them to take their stand upon the right to follow it wherever it might carry them). Then I have had them agree to read the gospel of John slowly and thoughtfully, and each time before they read to look up to God, if there were any God, to help them to understand what they were to read and to promise Him that they would take their stand upon whatever He showed them to be true and follow it wherever it would carry them. In every instance before they had finished the gospel, they had come to see that Jesus was the Christ, the Son of God, and have believed and been saved. They had put themselves in that position where the Holy Spirit could bear His testimony to Jesus Christ, and He had done it. Through His testimony they saw and believed.

If you wish men to see the truth about Christ, do not depend upon your own powers of expression and persuasion, but cast yourself upon the Holy Spirit, seek for them His testimony, and see to it that they put themselves in the place where the Holy Spirit can testify. This is the cure for both skepticism and ignorance concerning Christ. If you yourself are not clear concerning the truth about Jesus Christ, seek for yourself the testimony of the Holy Spirit regarding Christ. Read the Scriptures, read especially the gospel of John, but do not depend upon the mere reading of the Word. Before you read it, put yourself in such an attitude towards God by the absolute surrender of your will to Him that the Holy Spirit may bear His testimony in your heart concerning Jesus Christ. What we all most need is a clear and full vision of Jesus Christ, and this comes through the testimony of the Holy Spirit.

One night a number of our students came back from the Pacific Garden Mission in Chicago and said to me, "We had a wonderful meeting at the mission tonight. There were many drunkards and outcasts at the front who accepted Christ."

The next day I met Mr. Harry Monroe, the superintendent of the mission, on the street, and I said, "Harry, the boys say you had a wonderful meeting at the mission last night."

"Would you like to know how it came about?" he replied.

"Yes."

"Well," he said, "I simply held up Jesus Christ, and it so pleased the Holy Spirit to illumine the face of Jesus Christ that men saw and believed."

It was a unique way of putting it, but it was an expressive way and true to the essential facts in the case. It is our part to hold up Jesus Christ. We must then look to the Holy Spirit to illuminate His face or to take the truth about Him and make it clear to the hearts of our hearers. He will do it, and men will see and believe. Of course, we need to be so walking towards God that the Holy Spirit may take us as the instruments through whom He will bear His testimony.

Chapter 9

The Regenerating Work of the Holy Spirit

The apostle Paul writes, "Not by works of righteousness which we have done, but according to his mercy he saved us, by the washing of regeneration, and renewing of the Holy Ghost" (Titus 3:5). In these words we are taught that the Holy Spirit renews men, or makes men new, and that through this renewing of the Holy Spirit, we are saved. Jesus taught the same in John 3:3–5:

> Jesus answered and said unto him, Verily, verily, I say unto thee, Except a man be born again, he cannot see the kingdom of God. Nicodemus saith unto him, How can a man be born when he is old? can he enter the second time into his mother's womb, and be born? Jesus answered, Verily, verily, I say unto thee, Except a man be born of water and of the Spirit, he cannot enter into the kingdom of God.

What is regeneration? Regeneration is the impartation of life, spiritual life, to those who are dead, spiritually dead, through their trespasses and sins (Eph. 2:1). It is the Holy Spirit who imparts this life. It is true that the written Word is the instrument which the Holy Spirit uses in regeneration. We read in 1 Peter 1:23, "Being born again, not of corruptible seed, but of incorruptible, by the word of God, which liveth and abideth forever." We read in James 1:18, "Of his own will begat he us with the word of truth, that we should be a kind of first fruits of his creatures." These passages make it plain that the Word is the instrument used in regeneration, but it is only as the Holy Spirit uses the instrument that the new birth results. "It is the spirit that giveth life" (John 6:63 ASV).

In 2 Corinthians 3:6, we are told that "the letter killeth, but the spirit giveth life."[1] This is sometimes interpreted to mean that the literal interpretation of Scripture, the interpretation that takes it in its strict grammatical sense and makes it mean what it says, kills. It then means that some spiritual interpretation—an interpretation that "gives the spirit of the passage" by making it mean something it does not say—gives life, and those who insist upon Scripture meaning exactly what it says are called "deadly literalists." This is a favorite perversion of Scripture with those who do not like to take the Bible as meaning just what it says and who find themselves

---

[1] Both the translators of the Authorized Version (KJV) and the Revised Version (RV), and even the translators of the American Revision (ASV), seem to have lost sight of the context, for while they spell "Spirit" in the third verse with a capital, in the sixth verse in all three versions, it is spelled with a small "s."

driven into a corner looking about for some convenient way of escape. If one will read the words in their context, he will see that this thought was utterly foreign to the mind of Paul. Indeed, one who will carefully study the epistles of Paul will find that he himself was a literalist of the literalists.

If literalism is deadly, then the teachings of Paul are among the most deadly ever written. Paul built an argument upon the turn of a word, upon a number or a tense. What does the passage mean? The way to find out what any passage means is to study the words used in their context. Paul is drawing a contrast between the Word of God outside of us, written with ink upon parchment or engraved on tablets of stone, and the Word of God written within us in tablets that are hearts of flesh with the Spirit of the living God (2 Cor. 3:3). He tells us that if we merely have the Word of God outside us in a book or on parchment or on tablets of stone, that it will kill us, that it will only bring condemnation and death, but that if we have the Word of God made a living thing in our hearts, written upon our hearts by the Spirit of the living God, that it will bring us life.[2] No number of Bibles upon our tables or in our libraries will save us, but

[2] The ministry of many an orthodox preacher and teacher is a ministry of death. It is true that the message of the Gospel is preached, but it is preached with enticing words of man's wisdom and not in the demonstration of the Spirit and of power. (See 1 Corinthians 2:4.) The Gospel preached through this ministry of death comes in word only and not in power and the Holy Spirit. (See 1 Thessalonians 1:5.)

111

the truth of the Bible written by the Spirit of the living God in our hearts will save us.

To put the matter of regeneration in another way: regeneration is the impartation of a new nature, God's own nature, to the one who is born again. (See 2 Peter 1:4.) Every human being is born into this world with a perverted nature; his whole intellectual, emotional, and discretionary nature is perverted by sin. No matter how excellent our human ancestry, we come into this world with a mind that is blind to the truth of God: "The natural man receiveth not the things of the Spirit of God: for they are foolishness unto him: neither can he know them, because they are spiritually discerned" (1 Cor. 2:14). We come with affections that are alienated from God, loving the things that we ought to hate and hating the things that we ought to love:

> *Now the works of the flesh are manifest, which are these; Adultery, fornication, uncleanness, lasciviousness, idolatry, witchcraft, hatred, variance, emulations, wrath, strife, seditions, heresies, envyings, murders, drunkenness, revellings, and such like.*
> *(Gal. 5:19–21)*

We come with a will that is perverted, set upon pleasing itself, rather than pleasing God: "Because the carnal mind is enmity against God: for it is not subject to the law of God, neither indeed can be" (Rom. 8:7).

In the new birth a new intellectual, emotional, and discretionary nature is imparted to us. We receive the mind that sees as God sees, that thinks God's thoughts after Him. (See 1 Corinthians 2:12–14.) We receive affections in harmony with the affections of God: "The fruit of the Spirit is love, joy, peace, longsuffering, gentleness, goodness, faith, meekness, temperance: against such there is no law" (Gal. 5:22–23). We receive a will that is in harmony with the will of God, that delights to do the things that please Him. Like Jesus we say, "My meat is to do the will of him that sent me, and to finish his work" (John 4:34; compare John 6:38 and Galatians 1:10). It is the Holy Spirit who creates in us this new nature or imparts this new nature to us. No amount of preaching, no matter how orthodox it may be, and no amount of mere study of the Word will regenerate unless the Holy Spirit works. It is He and He alone who makes a man a new creature.

The new birth is compared in the Bible to growth from a seed. The human heart is the soil, "the seed is the word of God" (Luke 8:11; compare 1 Peter 1:23; James 1:18; and 1 Corinthians 4:15). Every preacher or teacher of the Word is a sower, but the Spirit of God is the One who quickens the seed that is thus sown. The divine nature then springs up as the result. There is abundant soil everywhere in which to sow the seed in the human hearts that are around about us. There is abundant seed to be sown; any of us can find it in the granary of God's Word. There are many sowers today, but unless as we sow the seed, the Spirit of God quickens it and the heart of the hearer closes around it by faith, there will be no harvest. Every sower needs to see to it that he realizes his dependence upon the Holy Spirit to quicken the seed he sows, and he needs to see to it also that he is in such relation to God that the Holy Spirit may work through him and quicken the seed he sows.

The Holy Spirit does regenerate men. He has power to raise the dead. He has power to impart life to those who are morally both dead and decaying. He has power to impart an entirely new nature to those whose nature now is so corrupt that to men they appear to be beyond hope. How often I have seen it proven. How often I have seen men and women utterly lost and ruined and vile come into a meeting scarcely knowing why they came. As they have sat there, the Word was spoken, the Spirit of God has quickened the Word thus sown in their hearts, and in a moment that man or woman, by the mighty power of the Holy Spirit, has become a new creation.

I know a man who seemed as completely abandoned and hopeless as men ever become. He was about forty-five years of age. He had gone off in evil courses in early boyhood. He had run away from home, had joined the navy and afterwards the army, and had learned all the vices of both. He had been dishonorably discharged from the army because of his extreme dissipation and disorderliness. He had found his companions among the lowest of the low and the vilest of the vile. When he would go up the street of a Western town at night, merchants would hear his yell and would close their doors in fear. This man went one night into a revival meeting in a country church out of curiosity. He made sport of the meeting that night with a boon companion who sat by his side, but he went again the next night. The Spirit of God touched his heart. He went forward and bowed at the altar. He arose a new creation. He was transformed into one of the noblest, truest, purest, most unselfish, most gentle, and most Christlike men I have ever known.

I am sometimes asked, "Do you believe in sudden conversion?" I believe in something far more wonderful than sudden conversion. I believe in sudden regeneration. Conversion is merely an outward thing, the turning around. Regeneration goes down to the deepest depths of the inmost soul, transforming thoughts, affections, will, the whole inward man. I believe in sudden regeneration because the Bible teaches it and because I have seen it times without number. I believe in sudden regeneration because I have experienced it. We are sometimes told that the religion of the future will not teach sudden, miraculous conversion. If the religion of the future does not teach sudden miraculous conversion, if it does not teach meaningful, sudden, and miraculous regeneration by the power of the Holy Spirit, then the religion of the future will not be in conformity with the facts of experience and will not be scientific. It will miss one of the most certain and most glorious of all truths.

Man-devised religions in the past have often missed the truth, and man-devised religions in the future will doubtless do the same. However, the religion God has revealed in His Word and that He confirms in experience teaches sudden regeneration by the mighty power of the Holy Spirit. If I did not believe in regeneration by the power of the Holy Spirit, I would quit preaching. What would be the use in facing great audiences in which there were multitudes of men and women hardened and seared, caring for nothing but the things of the world and the flesh, with no high and holy aspirations, with no outlook beyond money and fame and power and pleasure, if it were not for the regenerating power of the Holy Spirit?

But with the regenerating power of the Holy Spirit, there is every use, for the preacher can never tell where the Spirit of God is going to strike and do His mighty work. There sits before you a man who is a gambler or a drunkard or a philanderer. There does not seem to be much use in preaching to him. But you can never tell, that very night the Spirit of God may touch that man's heart and transform him into one of the holiest and most useful of men. It has often occurred in the past and will doubtless often occur in the future. There sits before you a woman who is a mere butterfly of fashion. She seems to have no thought above society and pleasure and adulation. Why preach to her? Without the regenerating power of the Holy Spirit, it would be foolishness and a waste of time. But you can never tell, perhaps this very night the Spirit of God will shine in that darkened heart and open the eyes of that woman to see the beauty of Jesus Christ, and she may receive Him. Then and there the life of God will be imparted by the power of the Holy Spirit to her trifling soul.

The doctrine of the regenerating power of the Holy Spirit is a glorious doctrine. It sweeps away false hopes. It comes to the one who is trusting in education and culture and says, "Education and culture are not enough. You must be born again." It comes to the one who is trusting in mere external morality and says, "External morality is not enough; you must be born again." It comes to the one who is trusting in the externalities of religion—in going to church, reading the Bible, saying prayers, being confirmed, being baptized, partaking of the Lord's supper—and says, "The mere externalities of religion are not enough; you must be born again." It comes to the one who is trusting in turning over a new leaf, in outward reform, in quitting his meanness; it says, "Outward reform, quitting your meanness is not enough. You must be born again." But in place of the vague and shallow hopes that it sweeps away, it brings in a new hope, a good hope, a blessed hope, a glorious hope. It says, "You may be born again." It comes to the one who has no desire higher than the desire for things animal or selfish or worldly and says, "You may become a partaker of the divine nature and love the things that God loves and hate the things that God hates. You may become like Jesus Christ. You may be born again."

Chapter 10

The Satisfaction Which Comes from the Indwelling Spirit

The Holy Spirit takes up His abode in the one who is born of the Spirit. The apostle Paul says to the believers in Corinth, "Know ye not that ye are the temple of God, and that the Spirit of God dwelleth in you?" (1 Cor. 3:16). This passage refers not so much to the individual believer as to the whole body of believers, the church. The church as a body is indwelt by the Spirit of God. But in 1 Corinthians 6:19, we read, "Know ye not that your body is the temple of the Holy Ghost which is in you, which ye have of God?" It is evident in this passage that Paul is not speaking of the body of believers, of the church as a whole, but of the individual believer. In a similar way, the Lord Jesus said to His disciples on the night before His crucifixion,

> And I will pray the Father, and he shall give you another Comforter, that he may abide with you for ever; Even the Spirit of truth; whom the world cannot receive, because it

seeth him not, neither knoweth him: but ye
know him; for he dwelleth with you, and
shall be in you.   (John 14:16–17)

The Holy Spirit dwells in everyone who is born again.

We read in Romans 8:9, "If any man have not the Spirit of Christ he is none of his." The Spirit of Christ in this verse, as we have already seen, does not mean merely a Christlike spirit but is a name of the Holy Spirit. One may be a very imperfect believer, but if he really is a believer in Jesus Christ, if he has really been born again, the Spirit of God dwells in him. It is very evident from the First Epistle to the Corinthians that the believers in Corinth were very imperfect believers; they were full of imperfection, and there was gross sin among them. Nevertheless, Paul tells them, even when dealing with them concerning gross immoralities, that they are temples of the Holy Spirit. (See 1 Corinthians 6:15–19.)

The Holy Spirit dwells in every child of God. In some, however, He dwells way back of consciousness in the hidden sanctuary of their spirits. He is not allowed to take possession as He desires of the whole man—spirit, soul, and body. Some, therefore, are not distinctly conscious of His indwelling, but He is there nonetheless. What a solemn, and yet, what a glorious thought, that in me dwells this august person, the Holy Spirit.

If we are children of God, we are not so much to pray that the Spirit may come and dwell in us, for He does that already. We are rather to recognize

His presence, His gracious and glorious indwelling, give to Him complete control of the house He already inhabits, and strive to so live as not to grieve this holy One, this divine Guest. We shall see later, however, that it is right to pray for the filling or baptism with the Spirit. What a thought it gives of the hallowedness and sacredness of the body to think of the Holy Spirit dwelling within us. How considerately we ought to treat these bodies and how sensitively we ought to shun everything that will defile them. How carefully we ought to walk in all things so as not to grieve Him who dwells within us.

This indwelling Spirit is a source of full and everlasting satisfaction and life. Jesus says in John 4:14, "Whosoever drinketh of the water that I shall give him shall never thirst; but the water that I shall give him shall be in him a well of water springing up into everlasting life." Jesus was talking to the woman of Samaria by the well at Sychar. She had said to Him, "Art thou greater than our father Jacob, which gave us the well, and drank thereof himself, and his children, and his cattle?" (John 4:12). Then Jesus answered and said to her, "Whosoever drinketh of this water shall thirst again" (John 4:13). How true that is of every earthly fountain. No matter how deeply we drink, we will thirst again.

No earthly spring of satisfaction ever fully satisfies. We may drink of the fountain of wealth as deeply as we may, but it will not satisfy for long. We will thirst again. We may drink of the fountain of fame as deeply as any man ever drank, yet the satisfaction is but for an hour. We may drink of the fountain of worldly pleasure, of human science and philosophy, and of earthly learning. We may even drink of the fountain of human love, but none will satisfy for long. We will thirst again.

Jesus went on to say, "But whosoever drinketh of the water that I shall give him shall never thirst; but the water that I shall give him shall be in him a well of water springing up into everlasting life" (John 4:14). The water that Jesus Christ gives is the Holy Spirit. This John tells us in the most explicit language:

> *In the last day, that great day of the feast, Jesus stood and cried, saying, If any man thirst, let him come unto me and drink. He that believeth on me, as the scripture hath said, out of his belly shall flow rivers of living water. But this spake he of the Spirit, which they that believe on him should receive.*   *(John 7:37–39)*

The Holy Spirit fully and forever satisfies the one who receives Him. He becomes within him a well of water springing up, ever springing up, into everlasting life. It is a great thing to have a well that you can carry with you; to have a well that is within you; to have your source of satisfaction, not in the things outside yourself, but in a well within and that is always within and that is always springing up in freshness and power; to have our well of satisfaction and joy within us. We are then independent of our environment. It matters little whether we have health or sickness, prosperity or adversity, our source of joy is within and is ever springing up. It matters comparatively little even whether we have our friends with us or are separated from them, separated even by what men call death. This fountain within is always gushing up, and our souls are satisfied.

Sometimes this fountain within gushes up with greatest power and fullness in the days of deepest bereavement. At such a time all earthly satisfactions fail. What satisfaction is there in money or worldly pleasure, in the theatre or the opera or the dance, in fame or power or human learning, when some loved one is taken from us? But in the hours when those that we loved most dearly upon earth are taken from us, then it is that the spring of joy of the indwelling Spirit of God bursts forth with fullest flow. Sorrow and sighing flee away, and our own spirits are filled with peace and ecstasy. We have "beauty for ashes, the oil of joy for mourning, the garment of praise for the spirit of heaviness" (Isa. 61:3). If the experience were not too sacred to put in print, I could tell of a moment of sudden and overwhelming bereavement and sorrow when it seemed as if I would be crushed, when I cried aloud in an agony that seemed unendurable, when suddenly and instantly this fountain of the Holy Spirit within burst forth, when I knew such a rest and joy as I had rarely known before, and my whole being was suffused with the oil of gladness.

The one who has the Spirit of God dwelling within as a well springing up into everlasting life is independent of the world's pleasures. He does not need to run after the theatre and the opera and the dance and the cards and the other pleasures without which life does not seem worth living to those who have not received the Holy Spirit. He gives these things up, not so much because he thinks they are wrong as because he has something so much better. He loses all taste for them.

A lady once came to Mr. Moody and said, "Mr. Moody, I do not like you."

He asked, "Why not?"

She said, "Because you are too narrow."

"Narrow! I did not know that I was narrow."

"Yes, you are too narrow. You don't believe in the theatre; you don't believe in cards; you don't believe in dancing."

"How do you know I don't believe in the theatre?" he asked.

"Oh," she said, "I know you don't."

Mr. Moody replied, "I go to the theatre whenever I want to."

"What," cried the woman, "you go to the theatre whenever you want to?"

"Yes, I go to the theatre whenever I want to."

"Oh," she said, "Mr. Moody, you are a much broader man than I thought you were. I am so glad to hear you say it, that you go to the theatre whenever you want to."

"Yes, I go to the theatre whenever I want to. I don't want to." Anyone who has really received the Holy Spirit, and in whom the Holy Spirit dwells and is unhindered in His working, will not want to. Why is it then that so many professed Christians do go after these worldly amusements? For one of two reasons: either because they have never definitely received the Holy Spirit or else because the fountain is choked. It is quite possible for a fountain to become choked. The best well in one of our inland cities was choked and dry for many months because an old rag carpet had been thrust into the opening from which the water flowed. When the rag was pulled out, the water flowed again, pure and cool and invigorating. There are many in the church today who once knew the matchless joy of the Holy Spirit, but some sin or worldly conformity, some act of disobedience, more or less conscious disobedience, to God has come in and the fountain is choked. Let us pull out the old rags today that this wondrous fountain may burst forth again, springing up every day and hour into everlasting life.

Chapter 11

The Holy Spirit Setting the Believer Free from the Power of Indwelling Sin

I n Romans 8:2 the apostle Paul writes, "The law of the Spirit of life in Christ Jesus hath made me free from the law of sin and death." We learn from Romans 7:9–24 what the law of sin and death is. Paul tells us that there was a time in his life when he was "alive without the law" (v. 9), but the time came when he was brought face to face with the law of God. He saw that this law was holy, and the commandment holy and just and good. And he made up his mind to keep this holy and just and good law of God. But he soon discovered that beside this law of God outside him, which was holy and just and good, there was another law inside him directly contrary to this law of God outside him. While the law of God outside him said, "This good thing" and "this good thing" and "this good thing" and "this good thing thou shalt do," the law within him said, "You cannot do this good thing that you would."

A fierce combat ensued between this holy and just and good law without him which Paul himself approved after the inward man, and this other law in his members which warred against the law of his mind and kept constantly saying, "You cannot do the good that you would." But this law in his members, the law that "the good that I would I do not: but the evil which I would not, that I do" (Rom. 7:19), gained the victory. Paul's attempt to keep the law of God resulted in total failure. He found himself sinking deeper and deeper into the mire of sin, constrained and dragged down by this law of sin in his members, until at last he cried out, "O, wretched man that I am! who shall deliver me out of the body of this death?" (Rom. 7:24).

Then Paul made another discovery. He found that in addition to the two laws that he had already found, the law of God outside of him, holy and just and good, and the law of sin and death within him, the law that the good he would he could not do and the evil he would not he must keep on doing, there was a third law: "the law of the Spirit of life in Christ Jesus" (Rom. 8:2). This law is about the righteousness which you cannot achieve in your own strength by the power of your own will approving the law of God, the righteousness which the law of God outside of you, holy and just and good though it is, cannot accomplish in you, in that it is weak through your flesh. The Spirit of life in Christ Jesus can produce this righteousness in you so "that the righteousness of the law might be fulfilled in us, who walk not after the flesh, but after the Spirit" (Rom. 8:4). In other words, when we come to the end of ourselves, when we fully realize our own inability to keep the law of God and in utter helplessness look up to the Holy Spirit in Christ Jesus to do for us that which we cannot do for ourselves, and when we surrender our every thought and every purpose and every desire and every affection to His absolute control and thus walk after the Spirit, the Spirit does take control and set us free from the power of sin that dwells in us and brings every hour of our lives into conformity to the will of God. It is the privilege of the child of God in the power of the Holy Spirit to have victory over sin every day and every hour and every moment.

There are many professed Christians today living in the experience that Paul described in Romans 7:9–24. Each day is a day of defeat, and at the close of the day, if they review their lives, they must cry as Paul did, "O, wretched man that I am! who shall deliver me out of the body of this death?" (Rom. 7:24). There are some who even go so far as to reason that this is the normal Christian life, but Paul tells us distinctly that this was "when the commandment came" (Rom. 7:9), not when the Spirit came, that it is the experience under law and not in the Spirit. The pronoun "I" occurs twenty-seven times in these fifteen verses and the Holy Spirit is not found once. Whereas in the eighth chapter of Romans the pronoun "I" is found only twice in the whole chapter, and the Holy Spirit appears constantly. Again Paul tells us in Romans 7:14 that this was his experience as "carnal, sold under sin." Certainly, that does not describe the normal Christian experience.

On the other hand, in Romans 8:9 we are told how not to be in the flesh but in the Spirit. In the eighth chapter of Romans, we have a picture of the true Christian life, the life that is possible to each one of us and that God expects from each one of us. Here we have a life where not merely the commandment comes but the Spirit comes and works obedience to the commandment and brings us complete victory over the law of sin and death. Here we have life, not in the flesh but in the Spirit, where we not only see the beauty of the law (see Romans 7:22) but where the Spirit imparts power to keep it (see Romans 8:4). We still have the flesh, but we are not in the flesh and do not live after the flesh. We "through the Spirit do mortify the deeds of the body" (Rom. 8:13). The desires of the body are still there, desires which, if made the rule of our lives, would lead us into sin. But day by day, by the power of the Spirit, we do put to death the deeds to which the desires of the body would lead us. We walk by the Spirit and therefore do not fulfill the lusts of the flesh (Gal. 5:16). We have crucified the flesh with the passions and lusts thereof (Gal. 5:24).

It would be going too far to say we still had a carnal nature for a carnal nature is a nature governed by the flesh. We have the flesh but in the Spirit's power, and it is our privilege to get daily, hourly, constant victory over the flesh and over sin. But this victory is not in ourselves, nor in any strength of our own. Left to ourselves, deserted of the Spirit of God, we would be as helpless as ever. It is still true that in us, that is in our flesh, "dwelleth no good thing" (Rom. 7:18). It is all in the power of the indwelling Spirit, but the Spirit's power may be in such fullness that one is not even conscious of the presence of the flesh. It seems as if it were dead and gone forever, but it is only kept in place of death by the Holy Spirit's power. If for one moment we were to take our eyes off of Jesus Christ, if we were to neglect the daily study of the Word and prayer, down we would go. We must live in the Spirit and walk in the Spirit if we would have continuous victory. (See Galatians 5:16, 25.) The life of the Spirit within us must be maintained by the study of the Word and prayer.

One of the saddest things ever witnessed is the way in which some people who have entered by the Spirit's power into a life of victory become self-confident and fancy that the victory is in themselves and that they can safely neglect the study of the Word and prayer. The depths to which such people sometimes fall is appalling. Each of us needs to take to heart the inspired words of the apostle, "Wherefore let him that thinketh he standeth take heed lest he fall" (1 Cor. 10:12).

I once knew a man who seemed to make extraordinary strides in the Christian life. He became a teacher of others and was a great blessing to thousands. It seemed to me that he was becoming self-confident, and I trembled for him. I invited him to my room, and we had a long heart-to-heart conversation. I told him frankly that it seemed as if he were going perilously near exceedingly dangerous ground. I said that I found it safer at the close of each day not to be too confident that there had been no failures or defeats that day but to go alone with God and ask Him to search my heart and show me if there was anything in my outward or inward life that was displeasing to Him. Very often failures were brought to light that must be confessed as sin.

"No," he replied, "I do not need to do that. Even if I should do something wrong, I would see it at once. I keep very short accounts with God, and I would confess it at once."

I said it seemed to me as if it would be safer to take time alone with God for God to search us through and through. While we might not know anything against ourselves, God might know something against us (see 1 Corinthians 4:4), and He would bring it to light. Our failure could be confessed and put away.

"No," he said he did not feel that was necessary. Satan took advantage of his self-confidence. He fell into most appalling sin, and though he has since confessed and professed repentance, he has been utterly set aside from God's service.

In John 8:32 we read, "Ye shall know the truth, and the truth shall make you free." In this verse it is the truth, or the Word of God, that sets us free from the power of sin and gives us victory. In Psalm 119:11 we read, "Thy word have I hid in mine heart, that I might not sin against thee." Here again it is the indwelling Word that keeps us free from sin. In this matter as in everything else, what in one place is attributed to the Holy Spirit is elsewhere attributed to the Word. The explanation, of course, is that the Holy Spirit works through the Word, and it is futile to talk of the Holy Spirit dwelling in us if we neglect the Word.

If we are not feeding on the Word, we are not walking after the Spirit, and we will not have victory over the flesh and over sin.

Chapter 12

The Holy Spirit Forming Christ within Us

It is a wonderful and deeply significant prayer that Paul offers in Ephesians for the believers in Ephesus and for all believers who read the epistle. Paul writes,

> For this cause I bow my knees unto the Father of our Lord Jesus Christ, Of whom the whole family in heaven and earth is named, That he would grant you, according to the riches of his glory, to be strengthened with might by his Spirit in the inner man; That Christ may dwell in your hearts by faith; that ye, being rooted and grounded in love, May be able to comprehend with all saints what is the breadth, and length, and depth, and height; And to know the love of Christ, which passeth knowledge, that ye might be filled with all the fulness of God.
>
> (Eph. 3:14–19)

We have here an advance in the thought over that which we have just been studying in the preceding chapter. It is the carrying out of the former work to its completion. Here the power of the Spirit manifests itself, not merely in giving us victory over sin but in four things: in Christ dwelling in our hearts; in our being rooted and grounded in love; in our being made strong to comprehend with all the saints what is the breadth, and length, and depth, and height and to know the love of Christ which passeth knowledge; and in our being "filled with all the fulness of God."

Christ dwelling in our hearts

The word translated "dwell" in this passage is a very strong word. It means literally, "to dwell down," "to settle," "to dwell deep." It is the work of the Holy Spirit to form the living Christ within us, dwelling deep down in the deepest depths of our being. We have already seen that this was a part of the significance of the name sometimes used of the Holy Spirit, "the Spirit of Christ." In Christ on the cross of Calvary, making an atoning sacrifice for sin, bearing the curse of the broken law in our place, we have Christ *for* us. But by the power of the Holy Spirit bestowed upon us by the risen Christ, we have Christ *in* us. Herein lies the secret of a Christlike life.

We hear a great deal in these days about doing as Jesus would do. Certainly we ought as Christians to live like Christ. "He that saith he abideth in him ought himself also so to walk, even as he walked" (1 John 2:6). But any attempt on our part to imitate Christ in our own strength will only result in utter disappointment and despair. There is nothing more futile that we can possibly attempt than to imitate Christ in the power of our own will. If we imagine that we succeed, it will be simply because we have a very incomplete knowledge of Christ. The more we study Him, and the more perfectly we understand His conduct, the more clearly will we see how far short we have come from imitating Him. But God does not demand of us the impossible; He does not demand of us that we imitate Christ in our own strength. He offers to us something infinitely better. He offers to form Christ in us by the power of His Holy Spirit. And when Christ is thus formed in us by the Holy Spirit's power, all we have to do is to let this indwelling Christ live out His own life in us, and then we will be like Christ without struggle and effort of our own.

A woman, who had a deep knowledge of the Word and a rare experience of the fullness that there is in Christ, stood one morning before a body of ministers as they plied her with questions. "Do you mean to say, Mrs. H——," one of the ministers asked, "that you are holy?" Quickly but very meekly and gently, the elect lady replied, "Christ in me is holy." No, we are not holy. To the end of our lives in and of ourselves we are full of weakness and failure, but the Holy Spirit is able to form within us the Holy One of God, the indwelling Christ. He will live out His life through us in all the humblest relations of life as well as in those relations of life that are considered greater. He will live out His life through the mother in the home, through the day-laborer in the pit, through the business man in his office—everywhere.

Our being rooted and grounded in love

In verse seventeen, Paul multiplies figures here. The first figure is taken from the tree shooting its roots down deep into the earth and taking fast hold upon it. The second figure is taken from a great building with its foundations laid deep in the earth on the rock. Paul therefore tells us that by the strengthening of the Spirit in the inward man we send the roots of our life down deep into the soil of love and also that the foundations of the superstructure of our character are built upon the rock of love. Love is the sum of holiness, "the fulfilling of the law" (Rom. 13:10). Love is what we all most need in our relations to God, to Jesus Christ, and to one another, and it is the work of the Holy Spirit to root and ground our lives in love. There is the most intimate relation between Christ being formed within us, or made to dwell in us, and our being rooted and grounded in love for Jesus Christ Himself is the absolutely perfect embodiment of divine love.

Our being made strong to comprehend with all the saints what is the breadth, and length, and depth, and height; and to know the love of Christ which passeth knowledge

It is not enough that we love, we must know the love of Christ, but that love passes knowledge. It is so broad, so long, so high, so deep, that no one can comprehend it. But we can "apprehend" (RV) it; we can lay hold upon it; we can make it our own; we can hold it before us as the object of our meditation, our wonder, and our joy. But it is only in the power of the Holy Spirit that we can thus apprehend it. The mind cannot grasp it at all in its own native strength. A man untaught and un-strengthened by the Spirit of God may talk about the love of Christ, he may write poetry about it, he may go into rhapsodies over it, but it is only words, words, words. There is no real apprehension. But the Spirit of God makes us strong to really appre-hend it in all its breadth, in all its length, in all its depth, and in all its height.

Our being "filled unto all the fulness of God"

There is a very important change between the Authorized (KJV) and Revised Version (RV). The KJV reads, "filled with all the fulness of God" (Eph. 3:19). The Revised Version reads more exactly, "filled unto all the fulness of God." It is no wonder that the translators of the KJV staggered at what Paul said and sought to tone down the full force of his words. To be filled with all the fullness of God would not be so wonderful, for it is an easy matter to fill a pint cup with all the fullness of the ocean, a single dip will do it. But it would be an impossi-bility indeed to fill a pint cup unto all the fullness of the ocean until all the fullness that there is in the ocean is in that pint cup. It is seemingly a more impossible task that the Holy Spirit under-takes to do for us, to fill us "unto all the fullness" of the infinite God, to fill us until all the intellectual and moral fullness that there is in God is in us.

This is the believer's destiny, we are "heirs of God, and joint-heirs with Christ" (Rom. 8:17). In other words, we are heirs of God to the extent that Jesus Christ is an heir of God; that is, we are heirs to all God is and all God has. It is the work of the Holy Spirit to apply to us that which is already ours in Christ. It is His work to make ours experientially all God has and all God is until the work is consummated in our being: "filled unto all the fulness of God." This is not the work of a moment, or a day, or a week, or a month, or a year, but the Holy Spirit day by day puts His hand, as it were, into the fullness of God and conveys to us what He has taken from there and puts it into us. Then again He puts His hand into the fullness that there is in God and conveys to us what is taken from there and puts it into us, and this wonderful process goes on day after day, and week after week, and month after month, and year after year, and never ends until we are "filled unto all the fulness of God."

Chapter 13

The Holy Spirit Bringing Forth Christlike Graces of Character in the Believer

There is a singular charm, a charm that one can scarcely explain, in the words of Paul in Galatians 5:22–23: "The fruit of the Spirit is love, joy, peace, longsuffering, gentleness [kindness], goodness, faith, meekness, temperance." What a catalog we have here of lovely moral characteristics. Paul tells us that they are the fruit of the Spirit; that is, if the Holy Spirit is given control of our lives, this is the fruit that He will bear. All real beauty of character, all real Christlikeness in us, is the Holy Spirit's work; it is His fruit. He produces it. He bears it, not we. It is well to notice that these graces are not said to be the *fruits* of the Spirit but the *fruit*. In other words, if the Spirit is given control of our lives, He will not bear one of these as fruit in one person and another as fruit in another person, but this will be the one fruit of many flavors that He produces in each one.

There is also a unity of origin running throughout all the multiplicity of manifestation. It is a beautiful life that is set forth in these verses. Every word is worthy of earnest study and profound meditation. Think of these words one by one: "love," "joy," "peace," "longsuffering," "kindness," "goodness," "faith" (or "faithfulness" RV; *faith* is the better translation if properly understood. The word is deeper than faithfulness. It is a real faith that results in faithfulness) "meekness," "temperance" (or a life under perfect control by the power of the Holy Spirit). We have here a perfect picture of the life of Jesus Christ Himself. Is not this the life that we all long for, the Christlike life? However, this life is not natural to us and is not attainable by us by any effort of what we are in ourselves. The life that is natural to us is set forth in the three preceding verses:

> *Now the works of the flesh are manifest, which are these, Adultery, fornication, uncleanness, lasciviousness, idolatry, witchcraft, hatred, variance, emulations, wrath, strife, seditions, heresies, envyings, murders, drunkenness, revellings, and such like.*
> *(Gal. 5:19–21)*

All these works of the flesh will not manifest themselves in each individual. Some will manifest themselves in one, others in others, but they have one common source, the flesh. If we live in the flesh, this is the kind of a life that we will live. It is the life that is natural to us. But when the indwelling Spirit is given full control in the one He inhabits, when we are brought to realize the utter badness of the flesh and give up in hopeless despair of ever attaining to anything in its power, when, in other words, we come to the end of ourselves and just give over the whole work of making us what we ought to be to the indwelling Holy Spirit, then and only then these holy graces of character which are set forth in Galatians 5:22–23 are His fruit in our lives. Do you wish these graces in your character and life? Do you really wish them? Then renounce self utterly and all its strivings after holiness, give up any thought that you can ever attain to anything really morally beautiful in your own strength, and let the Holy Spirit, who already dwells in you (if you are a child of God) take full control and bear His own glorious fruit in your daily life.

We get very much the same thought from a different point of view in Galatians 2:20:

> *I am crucified with Christ: nevertheless I live; yet not I, but Christ liveth in me: and the life which I now live in the flesh I live by the faith of the Son of God, who loved me, and gave himself up for me.*

We hear a great deal in these days about the ethical culture, which usually means the cultivation of the flesh until it bears the fruit of the Spirit. It cannot be done, no more than thorns can be made to bear figs and the bramble bush grapes. (See Luke 6:44 and Matthew 12:33.)

We also hear a great deal about character building. That may be all very well if you bear constantly in mind that the Holy Spirit must do the building, and even then it is not so much building as fruit-bearing. (See, however, 2 Peter 1:5–7.)

We also hear a great deal about cultivating graces of character, but we must always bear it clearly in mind that the way to cultivate true graces of character is by submitting ourselves utterly to the Spirit to do His work and bear His fruit. This is "sanctification of the Spirit" (1 Pet. 1:2; 2 Thess. 2:13). There is a sense, however, in which cultivating graces of character is right, namely, we look at Jesus Christ to see what He is and what we therefore ought to be. Then we look to the Holy Spirit to make us this that we ought to be and thus, "beholding as in a glass the glory of the Lord, are changed into the same image from glory to glory, even as by the Spirit of the Lord" (2 Cor. 3:18). Settle it, however, clearly and forever that the flesh can never bear this fruit, that you can never attain to these things by your own effort, that they are "the fruit of the Spirit."

Chapter 14

The Holy Spirit Guiding the Believer into Life as a Son

The apostle Paul writes in Romans 8:14, "For as many as are led by the Spirit of God, they are the sons of God." In this passage we see the Holy Spirit taking the conduct of the believer's life. A true Christian life is a personally conducted life, conducted at every turn by a divine person. It is the believer's privilege to be absolutely set free from all care and worry and anxiety as to the decisions which we must make at any turn of life. The Holy Spirit undertakes all that responsibility for us. A true Christian life is not one governed by a long set of rules outside of us but led by a living and ever-present person within us.

It is in this connection that Paul says, "For ye have not received the spirit of bondage again to fear" (Rom. 8:15). A life governed by rules outside of one's self is a life of bondage. There is always fear that we haven't made quite enough rules, and there is always the dread that in an unguarded moment we may have broken some of the rules which we have made. The life that many professed

Christians lead is one of awful bondage for they have put upon themselves a yoke more grievous to bear than that of the ancient Mosaic law concerning which Peter said to the Jews of his time, that "neither our fathers nor we were able to bear" (Acts 15:10).

Many Christians have a long list of self-made rules: "Thou shalt do this," and "Thou shalt do this," and "Thou shalt do this," and "Thou shalt not do that," and "Thou shalt not do that," and "Thou shalt not do that." If by any chance they break one of these self-made rules, or forget to keep one of them, they are at once filled with an awful dread that they have brought upon themselves the displeasure of God (and even sometimes imagine that they have committed the unpardonable sin). This is not Christianity; this is legalism. "Ye have not received the spirit of bondage again to fear" (Rom. 8:15); we have received the Spirit who gives us the place of sons.

Our lives should not be governed by a set of rules outside of us but by the loving Spirit of Adoption within us. We should believe the teaching of God's Word that the Spirit of God's Son dwells within us, and we should surrender the absolute control of our life to Him and look to Him to guide us at every turn of life. He will do it only if we surrender to Him to do it and trust Him to do it. If in a moment of thoughtlessness we go our own way instead of His, we will not be filled with an overwhelming sense of condemnation and of fear of an offended God, but we will go to God as our Father, confess our going astray, believe that

He forgives us fully because He says so (see 1 John 1:9), and go on light and happy of heart to obey Him and be led by His Spirit.

Being led by the Spirit of God does not mean for a moment that we will do things that the written Word of God tells us not to do. The Holy Spirit never leads men contrary to the Book of which He Himself is the Author. If there is some spirit that is leading us to do something that is contrary to the explicit teachings of Jesus or the apostles, we may be perfectly sure that this spirit who is leading us is not the Holy Spirit. This point needs to be emphasized in our day, for there are not a few who give themselves over to the leading of some spirit whom they say is the Holy Spirit but who is leading them to do things explicitly forbidden in the Word. We must always remember that many false spirits and false prophets are out in the world. (See 1 John 4:1.) There are many who are so anxious to be led by some unseen power that they are ready to surrender the conduct of their lives to any spiritual influence or unseen person. In this way, they open their lives to the conduct and malevolent influence of evil spirits to the utter wreck and ruin of their lives.

A man who made great professions of piety once came to me and said that the Holy Spirit was leading him and "a sweet Christian woman" whom he had met to contemplate marriage.

"Why," I said, in astonishment, "you already have one wife."

"Yes," he said, "but you know we are not congenial, and we have not lived together for years."

"Yes," I replied, "I know you have not lived together for years, and I have looked into the matter, and I believe that the blame for that lies largely at your door. In any event, she is your wife. You have no reason to suppose she has been untrue to you, and Jesus Christ explicitly teaches that if you marry another while she lives, you commit adultery." (See Luke 16:18.)

"Oh, but," the man said, "the Spirit of God is leading us to love one another and to see that we ought to marry one another."

"You lie, and you blaspheme," I replied. "Any spirit that is leading you to disobey the plain teaching of Jesus Christ is not the Spirit of God but some spirit of the devil."

This perhaps was an extreme case, but cases of essentially the same character are not rare. Many professed Christians seek to justify themselves in doing things which are explicitly forbidden in the Word by saying that they are led by the Spirit of God. Not long ago, I protested to the leaders in a Christian assembly where at each meeting many professed to speak with tongues in distinct violation of the teaching of the Holy Spirit through the apostle Paul in 1 Corinthians 14:27–28:

> *If any man speak in an unknown tongue, let it be by two, or at the most by three, and that by course; and let one interpret. But if there be no interpreter, let him keep silence in the church; and let him speak to himself, and to God.*

The defense that they made was that the Holy Spirit led them to speak several at a time and many in a single meeting and that they must obey the Holy Spirit. In such a case as this, they felt they were not subject to the Word.

The Holy Spirit never contradicts Himself. He never leads the individual to do that which in the written Word He has commanded us all not to do. Any leading of the Spirit must be tested by that which we know to be the leading of the Spirit in the Word. But while we need to be on our guard against the leading of false spirits, it is our privilege to be led by the Holy Spirit and to lead a life free from the bondage of rules and free from the anxiety that we will not go wrong, a life as children whose Father has sent an unerring Guide to lead them all the way. Those who are thus led by the Spirit of God are "sons of God." That is, they are not merely children of God, born it is true of the Father but immature, but they are the grown children, the mature children of God. They are no longer babes but sons.

The apostle Paul draws a contrast in Galatians 4:1–7 between the babe under the tutelage of the law and differing nothing from a servant and the full-grown son who is no more a servant but a son walking in joyous liberty. It sometimes seems as if comparatively few Christians today had really thrown off the bondage of law, rules outside themselves, and entered into the joyous liberty of sons.

Chapter 15

The Holy Spirit Bearing Witness to Our Sonship

One of the most precious passages in the Bible regarding the work of the Holy Spirit is found in Romans 8:15–16:

> *For ye have not received the spirit of bondage again to fear; but ye have received the Spirit of adoption, whereby we cry, Abba, Father. The Spirit itself beareth witness with our spirit, that we are the children of God.*

There are two witnesses to our sonship. First, our own spirits, taking God at His Word ("As many as received him, to them gave he power to become the sons of God," John 1:12), bear witness to our sonship. Our own spirits unhesitatingly affirm that what God says—that we are sons of God—is true because God says so. But there is another witness to our sonship, namely, the Holy Spirit. He bears witness together with our spirit. "Together with" is the force of the Greek used in this passage. It does not say that He bears witness to our spirit but "together with" it. How He does this is explained in Galatians 4:6: "Because ye are sons, God hath sent forth the Spirit of his Son into your hearts, crying, Abba, Father." When we have received Jesus Christ as our Savior and accepted God's testimony concerning Christ that through Him we have become sons, the Spirit of His Son comes into our hearts filling them with an over-whelming sense of sonship and crying through our hearts, "Abba, Father."

The natural attitude of our hearts towards God is not that of sons. We may call Him Father with our lips as when, for example, we repeat in a formal way the prayer that Jesus taught us, "Our Father, which art in heaven" (Matt. 6:9), but there is no real sense that He is our Father. Our calling Him so is mere words. We do not really trust Him. We do not love to come into His presence; we do not love to look up into His face with a sense of wonderful joy and trust because we are talking to our Father. We dread God. We come to Him in prayer because we think we ought to and perhaps we are afraid of what might happen if we did not. However, when the Spirit of His Son bears witness together with our spirits to our sonship, then we are filled and thrilled with the sense that we are sons. We trust Him as we never even trusted our earthly fathers. There is even less fear of Him than there was of our earthly fathers. Reverence there is and awe as well. But oh! Such a sense of wonderful childlike trust.

Notice when it is that the Spirit bears witness with our spirits that we are the children of God.

We have the order of experience in the order of the verses in Romans 8. First, we see the Holy Spirit setting us free from the law of sin and death. Consequently, the righteousness of the law is fulfilled in us who walk not after the law but after the Spirit (vv. 2–4). Next, we have the believer not minding the things of the flesh but the things of the Spirit (v. 5). Then, we have the believer day by day through the Spirit putting to death the deeds of the body (v. 13). Then, we have the believer led by the Spirit of God. Then and only then, we have the Spirit bearing witness to our sonship.

There are many seeking the witness of the Spirit to their sonship in the wrong place. They practically demand the witness of the Spirit to their sonship before they have even confessed their acceptance of Christ and certainly before they have surrendered their lives fully to the control of the indwelling Spirit of God. No, let us seek things in their right order. Let us accept Jesus Christ as our Savior and surrender to Him as our Lord and Master because God commands us to do so. Let us confess Him before the world because God commands that. (See Matthew 10:32–33; Romans 10:9–10.) Let us assert that our sins are forgiven, that we have eternal life, that we are sons of God because God says so in His Word, and we are unwilling to make God a liar by doubting Him. (See John 1:12; 5:24; Acts 10:43; 13:38–39; and 1 John 5:10–13.). Let us surrender our lives to the control of the Spirit of life, looking to Him to set us free from the law of sin and death. Let us set our minds not upon the things of the flesh but the things of the Spirit. Let us through the Spirit day by day put to death the deeds of the body. Let us give our lives up to be led by the Spirit of God in all things. Then, let us simply trust God to send the Spirit of His Son into our hearts filling us with a sense of sonship, crying, "Abba, Father," and He will do it.

God, our Father, longs that we would know and realize that we are His sons. He longs to hear us call Him "Father" from hearts that realize what they say and that trust Him without a fear or anxiety. He is our Father; He alone in all the universe realizes the fullness of meaning that there is in that wonderful word "Father," and it brings joy to Him to have us realize that He is our Father and to call Him so.

Some years ago there was a father in the state of Illinois who had a child who had been deaf and dumb from her birth. It was a sad day in that home when they came to realize that that little child was deaf and would never hear and, as they thought, would never speak. The father heard of an institution in Jacksonville, Illinois, where deaf children were taught to speak. He took this little child to the institution and put her in the superintendent's charge. After the child had been there some time, the superintendent wrote telling the father that he should come and visit his child. A day was appointed, and the child was told that her father was coming. As the hour approached, she sat up in the window, watching the gate for her father to pass through. The moment he entered the gate she saw him, ran down the stairs and out on the lawn, met him, looked up into his face, and lifted up her hands and said, "Papa." When that father heard the dumb lips of his child speak for the first time and frame that sweet word, "Papa," such a throb of joy passed through his heart that he literally fell to the ground and rolled upon the grass in ecstasy.

There is a Father who loves as no earthly father, who longs to have His children realize that they are children, and when we look up into His face and from a heart which the Holy Spirit has filled with a sense of sonship call Him "Abba [papa], Father," no language can describe the joy of God.

Chapter 16

The Holy Spirit as a Teacher

B ut the Comforter which is the Holy Ghost, whom the Father will send in my name, he shall teach you all things, and bring all things to your remembrance, whatsoever I have said unto you" (John 14:26). Our Lord Jesus said these words in His last conversation with His disciples before His crucifixion.

Here we have a twofold work of the Holy Spirit, teaching and bringing to remembrance the things which Christ had already taught. We will take them in the reverse order.

The Holy Spirit brings to remembrance the words of Christ.

This promise was made primarily to the apostles and is the guarantee of the accuracy of their report of what Jesus said, but the Holy Spirit does a similar work with each believer who expects it of Him and who looks to Him to do it. The Holy Spirit brings to our mind the teachings of Christ and of the Word just when we need them for either the necessities of our life or of our service. Many of us could tell of occasions when we were in great distress of soul or great questioning as to duty or great extremity as to what to say to one whom we were trying to lead to Christ or to help, and at that exact moment the very Scripture we needed— some passage it may be we had not thought of for a long time and quite likely of which we had never thought in this connection—was brought to mind. Who did it? The Holy Spirit did it. He is ready to do it even more frequently, if we only expect it of Him and look to Him to do it. It is our privilege every time we sit down beside an inquirer to point him to the way of life to look up to the Holy Spirit and say, "Just what shall I say to this inquirer? Just what Scripture shall I use?"

There is a deep significance in the fact that in the verse immediately following this precious promise Jesus says, "Peace I leave with you, my peace I give unto you" (John 14:27). It is by the Spirit bringing His words to remembrance and teaching us the truth of God that we obtain and abide in this peace. If we will simply look to the Holy Spirit to bring to mind Scripture just when we need it, and just the Scripture we need, we shall indeed have Christ's peace every moment of our lives.

One who was preparing for Christian work came to me in great distress. He said he must give up his preparation for he could not memorize the Scriptures. "I am thirty-two years old," he said, "and have been in business now for years. I have gotten out of the habit of study, and I cannot memorize anything." The man longed to be in his

Master's service and the tears stood in his eyes as he said it. "Don't be discouraged," I replied. "Take your Lord's promise that the Holy Spirit will bring His words to remembrance, learn one passage of Scripture, fix it firmly in your mind, then another and then another and look to the Holy Spirit to bring them to your remembrance when you need them." He went on with his preparation. He trusted the Holy Spirit. Afterwards he took up work in a very difficult field, a field where all sorts of error abounded. They would gather around him on the street like bees, and he would take his Bible and trust the Holy Spirit to bring to remembrance the passages of Scripture that he needed. The Holy Spirit did it. His adversaries were filled with confusion as he met them at every point with the sure Word of God, and many of the most hardened were won for Christ.

The Holy Spirit will teach us all things.

There is a still more explicit promise to this effect two chapters further on in John. Here Jesus says,

> *I have yet many things to say unto you, but ye cannot bear them now. Howbeit when he, the Spirit of truth, is come, he will guide you into all truth: for he shall not speak of himself; but whatsoever he shall hear, that shall he speak: and he will show you things to come. He shall glorify me: for he shall receive of mine, and shall show it unto you.*
> *(John 16:12–14)*

This promise was made in the first instance to the apostles, but the apostles themselves applied it to all believers. (See 1 John 2:20, 27.)

It is the privilege of each believer in Jesus Christ, even the humblest, to be "taught of God" (John 6:45). The humblest believer is independent of human teachers: "Ye need not that any man teach you" (1 John 2:27). This, of course, does not mean that we may not learn much from others who are taught of the Holy Spirit. If John had thought that, he would never have written this epistle to teach others. The man who is the most fully taught of God is the very one who will be most ready to listen to what God has taught others. Much less does it mean that when we are taught of the Spirit, we are independent of the written Word of God, for the Word is the very place to which the Spirit, who is the Author of the Word, leads His pupils and the instrument through which He instructs them. (See John 6:33; Ephesians 5:18–19; 6:17; and Colossians 3:16). But while we may learn much from men, we are not dependent upon them. We have a divine Teacher, the Holy Spirit.

We shall never truly know the truth until we are thus taught directly by the Holy Spirit. No amount of mere human teaching, no matter who our teachers may be, will ever give us a correct and exact and full apprehension of the truth. Not even a diligent study of the Word either in English or in the original languages will give us a real understanding of the truth. We must be taught directly by the Holy Spirit, and we may be thus taught, each one of us. The one who is thus taught will understand the truth of God better, even if he does not know one word of Greek or Hebrew, than the one who knows Greek and Hebrew thoroughly, and all the cognate languages as well, but who is not taught of the Spirit.

The Spirit will guide the one whom He thus teaches "into all truth" (John 16:13). The whole sphere of God's truth is for each one of us, but the Holy Spirit will not guide us into all the truth in a single day or in a week or in a year but step by step. There are two special areas of the Spirit's teaching mentioned:

"He will show you things to come." There are many who say we can know nothing of the future, that all our thoughts on that subject are guesswork. It is true that we cannot know everything about the future. There are some things which God has seen fit to keep to Himself, secret things which belong to Him. (See Deuteronomy 29:29). For example, we cannot "know the times or the seasons" (Acts 1:7) of our Lord's return, but there are many things about the future which the Holy Spirit will reveal to us.

"He shall glorify me [that is, Christ]: for he shall receive of mine and shall show it unto you." This is the Holy Spirit's special way of teaching the believer, as well as the unbeliever, about Jesus Christ. It is His work above all else to reveal Jesus Christ and to glorify Him. His whole teaching centers in Christ. From one point of view or the other, He is always bringing us to Jesus Christ. There are some who fear to emphasize the truth about the Holy Spirit lest Christ Himself be disparaged and put in the background, but there is no one who magnifies Christ as the Holy Spirit does. We shall never understand Christ, or see His glory, until the Holy Spirit interprets Him to us. No amount of listening to sermons and lectures, no matter how able, no amount of mere study of the Word even, would ever give us to see the things of Christ. The Holy Spirit must show us and is willing to do it and can do it. He is longing to do it. The Holy Spirit's most intense desire is to reveal Jesus Christ to men.

On the day of Pentecost when Peter and the rest of the company were "filled with the Holy Ghost" (Acts 2:4), they did not talk much about the Holy Spirit; they talked about Christ. Study Peter's sermon on that day. Jesus Christ was his one theme, and Jesus Christ will be our one theme if we are taught of the Spirit. Jesus Christ will occupy the whole horizon of our vision. We will have a new Christ, a glorious Christ. Christ will be so glorious to us that we will long to go and tell everyone about this glorious One whom we have found. Jesus Christ is so different when the Spirit glorifies Him by taking of His things and showing them to us.

The Holy Spirit reveals to us the deep things of God which are hidden from and are foolishness to the natural man.

Eye hath not seen, nor ear heard, neither have entered into the heart of man, the things which God hath prepared for them that love him. But God hath revealed them

157

unto us by his Spirit: for the Spirit searcheth all things, yea, the deep things of God. For what man knoweth the things of a man, save the spirit of man which is in him? even so the things of God knoweth no man, but the Spirit of God. Now we have received, not the spirit of the world, but the spirit which is of God; that we might know the things that are freely given to us of God. Which things also we speak, not in the words which man's wisdom teacheth, but which the Holy Ghost teacheth; comparing spiritual things with spiritual. (1 Cor. 2:9–13)

This passage, of course, refers primarily to the apostles, but we cannot limit this work of the Spirit to them. The Spirit reveals to the individual believer the deep things of God, things which human eye has not seen, nor ear heard, things which have not entered into the heart of man, the things which God has prepared for them that love Him. It is evident from the context that this does not refer solely to heaven or the things to come in the life hereafter. The Holy Spirit takes the deep things of God which God has prepared for us, even in the life that now is, and reveals them to us.

The Holy Spirit interprets His own revelation. He imparts power to discern, know, and appreciate what He has taught.

In the next verse to those just quoted we read, "But the natural man receiveth not the things of the Spirit of God: for they are foolishness unto him: neither can he know them, because they are spiritually discerned" (1 Cor. 3:14). Not only is the Holy Spirit the author of revelation, the written Word of God, He is also the interpreter of what He has revealed. Any profound book is immeasurably more interesting and helpful when we have the author of the book right at hand to interpret it to us, and it is always our privilege to have the author of the Bible right at hand when we study it. The Holy Spirit is the author of the Bible, and He stands ready to interpret its meaning to every believer every time he opens the Book. To understand the Book, we must look to Him, then the darkest places become clear. We often need to pray with the psalmist of old: "Open thou mine eyes, that I may behold wondrous things out of thy law" (Ps. 119:18).

It is not enough that we have the revelation of God before us in the written Word to study, we must also have the inward illumination of the Holy Spirit to enable us to apprehend it as we study. It is a common mistake, but a most palpable mistake, to try to comprehend a spiritual revelation with the natural understanding. It is the foolish attempt to do this that has landed so many in the bog of so-called "higher criticism." In order to understand art, a man must have aesthetic sense as well as the knowledge of colors and of paint, and to understand a spiritual revelation, a man must be taught of the Spirit. A mere knowledge of the languages in which the Bible was written is not enough. A man with no aesthetic sense might as well expect to appreciate the Sistine Madonna, because he is not color blind, as a man who is not filled with the Spirit to understand the Bible, simply because he understands the vocabulary and the laws of grammar of the languages in which the Bible was written. We might as well think of setting a man to teach art because he understood paints as to set a man to teach the Bible because he has a thorough understanding of Greek and Hebrew. In our day we need not only to recognize the utter insufficiency and worthlessness before God of our own righteousness, which is the lesson of the opening chapters of the epistle to the Romans, but also the utter insufficiency and worthlessness in the things of God of our own wisdom, which is the lesson of the First Epistle to the Corinthians, especially the first three chapters. (See, for example, 1 Corinthians 1:19–21, 26–27.)

The Jews of old had a revelation by the Spirit, but they failed to depend upon the Spirit Himself to interpret it to them, so they went astray. So Christians today have a revelation by the Spirit, and many are failing to depend upon the Holy Spirit to interpret it to them and so go astray. The whole evangelical church recognizes theoretically at least the utter insufficiency of man's own righteousness. What it needs to be taught in the present hour, and what it needs to be made to feel, is the utter insufficiency of man's wisdom. That is perhaps the lesson which this twentieth century of towering intellectual conceit needs most of all to learn.

To understand God's Word, we must empty ourselves utterly of our own wisdom and rest in utter dependence upon the Spirit of God to interpret it to us. We do well to take to heart the words of Jesus Himself in Matthew 11:25: "I thank thee, O Father, Lord of heaven and earth, because thou hast hid these things from the wise and prudent, and hast revealed them unto babes."

A number of Bible students were once discussing the best methods of Bible study. One man, who was in point of fact a learned and scholarly man, said, "I think the best method of Bible study is the baby method." When we have entirely put away our own righteousness, then and only then, we get the righteousness of God. (See Romans 10:3; Philippians 3:4–7, 9). When we have entirely put away our own wisdom, then and only then we get the wisdom of God. "Let no man deceive himself," says the apostle Paul, "If any man among you seemeth to be wise in this world, let him become a fool, that he may be wise" (1 Cor. 3:18). The emptying must precede filling, the self poured out that God may be poured in.

We must daily be taught by the Spirit to understand the Word. We cannot depend today on the fact that the Spirit taught us yesterday. Each new time that we come in contact with the Word, it must be in the power of the Spirit for that specific occasion. That the Holy Spirit once illumined our minds to grasp a certain truth is not enough. He must do it each time we confront that passage. Andrew Murray has well said, "Each time you come to the Word in study, in hearing a sermon, or reading a religious book, there ought to be as distinct as your intercourse with the external means, the definite act of self-abnegation, denying your own wisdom and yielding yourself in faith to the divine Teacher" (*The Spirit of Christ*).

The Holy Spirit enables the believer to communicate to others in power the truth he himself has been taught.

Paul says in 1 Corinthians 2:1–5,

And I, brethren, when I came to you, came not with excellency of speech or of wisdom, declaring unto you the testimony of God. For I determined not to know anything among you, save Jesus Christ, and him crucified. And I was with you in weakness, and in fear, and in much trembling. And my speech and my preaching was not with enticing words of man's wisdom, but in demonstration of the Spirit and of power: That your faith should not stand in the wisdom of men, but in the power of God.

In a similar way in writing to the believers in Thessalonica in 1 Thessalonians 1:5: "For our gospel came not unto you in word only, but also in power, and in the Holy Ghost, and in much assurance; as ye know what manner of men we were among you for your sake."

We not only need the Holy Spirit to reveal the truth to chosen apostles and prophets in the first place and in the second place to interpret to us as individuals the truth He has thus revealed, but in the third place, we need the Holy Spirit to enable us to effectually communicate to others the truth which He Himself has interpreted to us. We need Him all along the line. One great cause of real failure in the ministry, even when there is seeming success—not only in the regular ministry but in all forms of service as well—comes from the attempt to teach by "enticing words of man's wisdom" (1 Cor. 2:4), that is, by the arts of human logic, rhetoric, persuasion, and eloquence what the Holy Spirit has taught us. What is needed is Holy Ghost power, "demonstration of the Spirit and of power" (1 Cor. 2:4).

There are three causes of failure in preaching today. First, some other message is taught than the message which the Holy Spirit has revealed in the Word. Men preach science, art, literature, philosophy, sociology, history, economics, experience, etc., and not the simple Word of God as found in the Holy Spirit's Book, the Bible. Second, the Spirit-taught message of the Bible is studied and sought to be apprehended by the natural understanding, that is, without the Spirit's illumination. How common that is even in institutions where men are being trained for the ministry, even institutions which may be altogether orthodox. Third, the Spirit-given message, the Word, studied and apprehended under the Holy Ghost's illumination is given out to others with "enticing words of man's wisdom" and not in "demonstration of the Spirit and of power" (1 Cor. 2:4). We need, and are absolutely dependent upon, the Spirit all along the line. He must teach us how to speak as well as what to speak. His must be the power as well as the message.

Chapter 17

Praying, Returning Thanks, Worshipping in the Holy Spirit

Two of the most deeply significant passages in the Bible on the subject of the Holy Spirit and on the subject of prayer are found in Jude 1:20 and Ephesians 6:18. In Jude 1:20 we read, "But ye, beloved, building up yourselves on your most holy faith, praying in the Holy Ghost," and in Ephesians 6:18, "Praying always with all prayer and supplication in the Spirit, and watching thereunto with all perseverance and supplication for all saints." These passages distinctly teach us three things.

The Holy Spirit guides the believer in prayer.

The disciples did not know how to pray as they ought so they came to Jesus and said, "Lord, teach us to pray" (Luke 11:1). We today do not know how to pray as we ought—we do not know what to pray for, nor how to ask for it—but there is One who is always at hand to help (see John 14:16–17), and He knows what we should pray for. He helps our infirmity in this matter of prayer as in other matters (Rom. 8:26). He teaches us to pray. True prayer is prayer in the Spirit (i.e., the prayer that the Holy Spirit inspires and directs).

The prayer in which the Holy Spirit leads us is the prayer "according to the will of God" (Rom. 8:27). When we ask anything according to God's will, we know that He hears us, and we know that He has granted the things that we ask. (See 1 John 5:14–15.) We may know it is ours at the moment when we pray just as surely as we know it afterwards when we have it in our actual possession. But how can we know the will of God when we pray? In two ways. First of all, by what is written in His Word. All the promises in the Bible are sure, and if God promises anything in the Bible, we may be sure it is His will to give us that thing. But there are many things that we need which are not specifically promised in the Word and still even in that case it is our privilege to know the will of God, for it is the work of the Holy Spirit to teach us God's will and lead us out in prayer along the line of God's will.

Some object to the Christian doctrine of prayer, for they say that it teaches that we can go to God in our ignorance and change His will and subject His infinite wisdom to our erring foolishness, but that is not the Christian doctrine of prayer at all. The Christian doctrine of prayer is that it is the believer's privilege to be taught by the Spirit of God Himself to know what the will of God is and not to ask for the things that our foolishness would prompt us to ask for but to ask for things that the never-erring Spirit of God prompts us to ask for. True prayer is prayer "in the Spirit"

(Eph. 6:18), that is, the prayer which the Spirit inspires and directs.

When we come into God's presence, we should recognize our infirmities: our ignorance of what is best for us, our ignorance of what we should pray for, and our ignorance of how we should pray for it. In the consciousness of our utter inability to pray correctly, we should look up to the Holy Spirit to teach us to pray and cast ourselves utterly upon Him to direct our prayers and to discover our desires and guide our utterance of them. There is no place where we need to recognize our ignorance more than we do in prayer. Rushing heedlessly into God's presence and asking the first thing that comes into our minds, or that some other thoughtless one asks us to pray for, is not praying "in the Holy Ghost" (Jude 1:20) and is not true prayer. We must wait for the Holy Spirit and surrender ourselves to Him. The prayer that God the Holy Spirit inspires is the prayer that God the Father answers.

The longings which the Holy Spirit begets in our hearts are often too deep for utterance, too deep apparently for clear and definite comprehension on the part of the believer himself in whom the Spirit is working: "The Spirit itself maketh intercession for us with groanings which cannot be uttered" (Rom. 8:26). God Himself "searcheth the hearts" to know what "the mind of the Spirit" is (Rom. 8:27) in these unuttered and unutterable longings. But God does know what the mind of the Spirit is. He does know what these Spirit-given longings which we cannot put into words mean even if we do not. These longings are "according to the will of God" (Rom. 8:27), and God grants them. It is in this way that it comes to pass that God "is able to do exceeding abundantly above all that we ask or think, according to the power that worketh in us (Eph. 3:20). There are other times when the Spirit's leadings are so clear that we pray with the Spirit and with the understanding also (1 Cor. 14:15). We distinctly understand what it is that the Holy Spirit leads us to pray for.

The Holy Spirit inspires the believer and guides him in thanksgiving as well as in prayer.

> *And be not drunk with wine, wherein is excess, but be filled with the Spirit; Speaking to yourselves in psalms and hymns and spiritual songs, singing and making melody in your heart to the Lord; Giving thanks always for all things unto God and the Father in the name of our Lord Jesus Christ.* (Eph. 5:18–20)

Not only does the Holy Spirit teach us to pray, He also teaches us to render thanks. One of the most prominent characteristics of the Spirit-filled life is thanksgiving. On the Day of Pentecost when the disciples were filled with the Holy Spirit and spoke as the Spirit gave them utterance, we hear them telling the wonderful works of God (Acts 2:4, 11). Today when any believer is filled with the Holy Spirit, he always becomes filled with thanksgiving and praise. True thanksgiving is "unto God and the Father," through or "in the name of our Lord Jesus Christ," in the Holy Spirit.

The Holy Spirit inspires worship on the part of the believer.

We read in Philippians 3:3 (RV), "For we are the circumcision, who worship by the Spirit of God, and glory in Christ Jesus, and have no confidence in the flesh." Prayer is not worship; thanksgiving is not worship. Worship is a definite act of the creature in relation to God. Worship is bowing before God in adoring acknowledgment and contemplation of Himself and the perfection of His being. Someone has said, "In our prayers, we are taken up with our needs; in our thanksgiving, we are taken up with our blessings; in our worship, we are taken up with Himself." There is no true and acceptable worship except that which the Holy Spirit prompts and directs. "God is a Spirit: and they that worship him must worship him in spirit and in truth...for the Father seeketh such to worship him" (John 4:24, 23). The flesh seeks to intrude into every sphere of life. The flesh has its worship as well as its lusts. The worship which the flesh prompts is an abomination to God. In this we see the folly of any attempt at a conference of religions where the representatives of radically different religions attempt to worship together.

Not all earnest and honest worship is worship in the Spirit. A man may be very honest and very earnest in his worship and still not have submitted himself to the guidance of the Holy Spirit in the matter, and so his worship is in the flesh. Oftentimes even when there is great loyalty to the letter of the Word, worship may not be in the Spirit—in other words, inspired and directed by Him. To worship aright, as Paul puts it, we must have "no confidence in the flesh" (Phil. 3:3); that is, we must recognize the utter inability of the flesh (our natural self as contrasted to the divine Spirit that dwells in and should mold everything in the believer) to worship acceptably. And we must also realize the danger that exists that the flesh may intrude itself into our worship. In utter self-distrust and self-abnegation, we must cast ourselves upon the Holy Spirit to lead us rightly in our worship. Just as we must renounce any merit in ourselves and cast ourselves upon Christ and His work for us upon the cross for justification, so we must renounce any supposed capacity for good in ourselves and cast ourselves utterly upon the Holy Spirit and His work in us, in holy living, knowing, praying, thanking, worshipping, and all else that we are to do.

Chapter 18

The Holy Spirit Sending Men Forth to Definite Lines of Work

As they ministered to the Lord, and fasted, the Holy Ghost said, Separate Me Barnabas and Saul for the work whereunto I have called them. And when they had fasted and prayed, and laid their hands on them, they sent them away. So they, being sent forth by the Holy Ghost, departed into Seleucia; and from thence they sailed to Cyprus" (Acts 13:2–4). It is evident from this passage that the Holy Spirit calls men into definite lines of work and sends them forth into the work. He not only calls men in a general way into Christian work but selects the specific work and points it out.

Many a Christian is asking today, and many others ought to ask, "Shall I go to China, to Africa, to India?" There is only one person who can rightly settle that question for you, and that person is the Holy Spirit. You cannot settle the question for yourself, much less can any other man settle it rightly for you. Not every Christian man is called to go to China; not every Christian man is called to go to Africa; not every Christian man is called to go to the foreign field at all. God alone knows whether He wishes you in any of these places, but He is willing to show you. In a day such as we live in, when there is such a need of the right men and the right women on the foreign field, every young and healthy and intellectually competent Christian man and woman should definitely offer themselves to God for the foreign field and ask Him if He wants them to go, but they ought not to go until He, by His Holy Spirit, makes it plain.

The great need in all areas of Christian work today is men and women whom the Holy Ghost calls and sends forth. We have plenty of men and women whom men have called and sent forth. We have plenty of men and women who have called themselves, for there are many today who object strenuously to being sent forth by men or by any organization of any kind. But, in fact, these men and women who are sent forth by themselves and not by God are immeasurably worse.

How does the Holy Spirit call? The passage before us does not tell us how the Holy Spirit spoke to the group of prophets and teachers in Antioch, telling them to separate Barnabas and Saul to the work to which He had called them. It is presumably purposely silent on this point. Possibly it is silent on this point lest we should think that the Holy Spirit must always call in precisely the same way. There is nothing whatsoever to indicate that He spoke by an audible voice. Much less is there anything to indicate that He made His will known in any of the fantastic ways in which some in these days profess to discern His leading—as for example, by twitchings of the body, by shuddering, by opening the Bible at random and putting a finger on a passage that may be construed into some entirely different meaning than that which the inspired author intended by it. The important point is, He made His will clearly known, and He is willing to make His will clearly known to us today. Sometimes He makes it known in one way and sometimes in another, but He will make it known.

But how do we receive the Holy Spirit's call? First of all, by desiring it; second, by earnestly seeking it; third, by waiting upon the Lord for it; fourth, by expecting it. The record reads, "As they ministered to the Lord, and fasted" (Acts 13:2). They were waiting upon the Lord for His direction. For the time being, they had turned their backs utterly upon worldly cares and enjoyments, even upon those things which were perfectly proper in their places.

Many a man is saying today to justify his staying home from the foreign field, "I have never had a call." How do you know that? Have you been listening for a call? God usually speaks in a still small voice, and it is only the listening ear that can catch it. Have you ever definitely offered yourself to God to send you where He will? While no man or woman ought to go to China or Africa or other foreign field unless they are clearly and definitely called, they ought each to offer themselves to God for this work and be ready for the call and be listening sharply so that they may hear the call if it comes. Let it be borne distinctly in mind that a man needs no more definite call to Africa than to Boston, or New York, or London, or any other desirable field at home.

The Holy Spirit not only calls men and sends them forth into definite areas of work, but He also guides in the details of daily life and service as to where to go and where not to go, what to do and what not to do. We read in Acts 8:27–29:

> *And he* [Philip] *arose and went: and, behold, a man of Ethiopia, an eunuch of great authority under Candace queen of the Ethiopians, who had the charge of all her treasure, and had come to Jerusalem for to worship, Was returning, and sitting in his chariot read Esaias* [Isaiah] *the prophet. Then the Spirit said unto Philip, Go near, and join thyself to this chariot.*

Here we see the Spirit guiding Philip in the details of service into which He had called him. In a similar way, we read in Acts 16:6–7 (RV):

> *And they went through the region of Phrygia and Galatia, having been forbidden of the Holy Ghost to speak the word in Asia; and when they were come over against Mysia, they assayed to go into Bithynia; and the Spirit of Jesus suffered them not.*

Here we see the Holy Spirit directing Paul where not to go.

It is possible for us to have the unerring guidance of the Holy Spirit at every turn of life. Take, for example, our personal work. It is manifestly not God's intention that we speak to everyone we meet. To attempt to do so would be to attempt the impossible, and we would waste much time in trying to speak to people where we could do no good that might be used in speaking to people where we could accomplish something. There are some to whom it would be wise for us to speak. There are others to whom it would be unwise for us to speak. Time spent on them would be taken from work that would be more to God's glory. Doubtless as Philip journeyed towards Gaza, he met many before he met the one of whom the Spirit said, "Go near, and join thyself to this chariot" (Acts 8:29). The Spirit is as ready to guide us as He was to guide Philip.

Some years ago, a Christian worker in Toronto had the impression that he should go to the hospital and speak to someone there. He thought to himself, "Whom do I know at the hospital at this time?" There came to his mind one whom he knew was at the hospital, and so he hurried there. But as he sat down by his side to talk with him, he realized it was not for this man that he was sent. He got up to lift a window. What did it all mean? There was another man lying across the aisle in the ward from the man he knew, and the thought came to him that this might be the man to whom he should speak. He turned and spoke to this man and had the privilege of leading him to Christ. There was apparently nothing serious in the man's case. He had suffered some injury to his knee and there was no thought of a serious issue, but that man passed into eternity that night.

Many instances of a similar character could be recorded and prove from experience that the Holy Spirit is as ready to guide those who seek His guidance today as He was to guide the early disciples. He is ready to guide us, not only in our more definite forms of Christian work but in all the affairs of life, business, study, and everything we have to do. There is no promise in the Bible more plainly explicit than the following:

> *If any of you lack wisdom, let him ask of God, that giveth to all men liberally, and upbraideth not; and it shall be given him. But let him ask in faith, nothing wavering. For he that wavereth is like a wave of the sea driven with the wind and tossed. For let not that man think that he shall receive any thing of the Lord.* (James 1:5–7)

This passage not only promises God's wisdom but tells us specifically just what to do to obtain it. There are really five steps stated or implied in the passage.

That we "lack wisdom"

We must be conscious of and fully admit our own inability to decide wisely. Here is where we often fail to receive God's wisdom. We think we are able to decide for ourselves or at least we are not ready to admit our own utter inability to decide.

There must be an entire renunciation of the wisdom of the flesh.

We must really desire to know God's way and be willing at any cost to do God's will.

This is implied in the word, "ask." The asking must be sincere, and if we are not willing to do God's will, whatever it may be, at any cost, the asking is not sincere. This is a point of fundamental importance. There is nothing that goes so far to make our minds clear in the discernment of the will of God as revealed by His Spirit as an absolutely surrendered will. Here we find the reason why men oftentimes do not know God's will and do not have the Spirit's guidance. They are not willing to do whatever the Spirit leads at any cost. It is he who wants to do His will who will know not only of the doctrine but his daily duty. Men oftentimes come to me and say, "I cannot find out the will of God," but when I put to them the question, "Are you willing to do the will of God at any cost?" they admit that they are not. The way that is very obscure when we hold back from an absolute surrender to God becomes as clear as day when we make that surrender.

We must definitely "ask" for guidance.

It is not enough to desire; it is not enough to be willing to obey; we must ask, definitely ask, God to show us the way.

We must confidently expect guidance.

"Let him ask in faith, nothing wavering" (James 1:6). There are many who cannot find the way, though they ask God to show it to them, simply because they have not the absolutely undoubting expectation that God will show them the way. God promises to show it if we expect it confidently. When you come to God in prayer to show you what to do, know for a certainty that He will show you. In what way He will show you, He does not tell, but He promises that He will show you and that is enough.

We must follow step-by-step as the guidance comes.

As said before, just how it will come, no one can tell, but it will come. Oftentimes only a step will be made clear at a time; that is all we need to know—the next step. Many are in darkness because they do not know and cannot find what God would have them do next week or next month or next year.

A college man once came to me and told me that he was in great darkness about God's guidance, that he had been seeking to find the will of God and learn what his life's work should be, but he could not find it. I asked him how far along he was in his college course. He said his sophomore year. I asked, "What is it you desire to know?"

"What I shall do when I finish college."

"Do you know that you ought to go through college?"

"Yes."

This man not only knew what he ought to do next year but the year after, but still he was in great perplexity because he did not know what he ought to do when these two years were ended. God delights to lead His children a step at a time. He leads us as He led the children of Israel:

> And when the cloud was taken up from the tabernacle, then after that the children of Israel journeyed: and in the place where the cloud abode, there the children of Israel pitched their tents. At the commandment of the LORD the children of Israel journeyed, and at the commandment of the LORD they pitched: as long as the cloud abode upon the tabernacle they rested in their tents. And when the cloud tarried long upon the tabernacle many days, then the children of Israel kept the charge of the LORD, and journeyed not. And so it was, when the cloud was a few days upon the tabernacle; according to the commandment of the LORD they abode in their tents, and according to the commandment of the LORD they journeyed. And so it was, when the cloud abode from even unto the morning, and that the cloud was taken up in the morning, then they journeyed: whether it was by day or by night that the cloud was taken up, they journeyed. Or whether it were two days, or a month, or a year, that the cloud tarried upon the tabernacle, remaining thereon, the children of Israel abode in their tents, and journeyed not:

but when it was taken up, they journeyed. At
the commandment of the LORD they rested in
the tents, and at the commandment· of the
LORD they journeyed: they kept the charge of
the LORD, at the commandment of the LORD
by the hand of Moses.   *(Num. 9:17–23)*

Many who have given themselves up to the
leading of the Holy Spirit get into a place of great
bondage and are tortured because they have leadings which they fear may be from God but of
which they are not sure. If they do not obey these
leadings, they are fearful they have disobeyed God
and sometimes imagine that they have grieved
away the Holy Spirit because they did not follow
His leading. This is all unnecessary. Let us settle it
in our minds that God's guidance is clear guidance. "God is light, and in him is no darkness at
all" (1 John 1:5). Any leading that is not perfectly
clear is not from Him, that is, if our wills are absolutely surrendered to Him. Of course, the uncer-
tainty may arise from an unsurrendered will. But
if our wills are absolutely surrendered to God, we
have the right as God's children to be sure that
any guidance is from Him before we obey it.

We have a right to go to our Father and say,
"Heavenly Father, here I am. I desire above all
things to do Your will. Now make it clear to me,
Your child. If this thing that I have a leading to do
is Your will, I will do it, but make it clear as day if
it is Your will." If it is His will, the heavenly Father will make it as clear as day. You need not and
ought not do that thing until He does make it
clear, and you need not and ought not condemn

yourself because you did not do it. God does not want His children to be in a state of condemnation before Him. He wishes us to be free from all care, worry, anxiety, and self-condemnation. Any earthly parent would make the way clear to his child that asked to know it, and much more will our heavenly Father make it clear to us. Until He does make it clear, we need have no fears that in not doing it we are disobeying God. We have no right to dictate to God as to how He should give His guidance—as, for example, by asking Him to shut up every way, by asking Him to give a sign, by guiding us in putting our finger on a text, or in any other way. It is ours to seek and to expect wisdom, but it is not ours to dictate how it will be given. The Holy Spirit divides to "every man severally as he will" (1 Cor. 12:11).

Two things are evident from what has been said about the work of the Holy Spirit: first, how utterly dependent we are upon the work of the Holy Spirit at every turn of Christian life and service; second, how perfect is the provision for life and service that God has made. How wonderful is the fullness of privilege that is open to the humblest believer through the Holy Spirit's work. It is not so much what we are by nature—either intellectually, morally, physically, or even spiritually—that is important. The important matter is what the Holy Spirit can do for us and what we will let Him do. Not infrequently, the Holy Spirit takes the one who seems to have the least natural promise and uses him far beyond those who have the greatest natural promise. Christian life is not to be lived in the realm of natural temperament, and Christian work is not to be done in the power of natural endowment. Christian life is to be lived in the realm of the Spirit, and Christian work is to be done in the power of the Spirit. The Holy Spirit is willing and eagerly desirous of doing for each one of us His whole work, and He will do in each one of us all that we will let Him do.

Chapter 19

The Holy Spirit and the Believer's Body

The Holy Spirit does a work for our bodies as well as for our minds and hearts. We read in Romans 8:11, "But if the Spirit of him that raised up Jesus from the dead dwell in you, he that raised up Christ from the dead shall also quicken your mortal bodies by his Spirit that dwelleth in you."

The Holy Spirit quickens the mortal body of the believer. It is very evident from the context that this refers to the future resurrection of the body. (See Romans 8:21–23.) The resurrection of the body is the Holy Spirit's work. The glorified body is from Him; it is "a spiritual body" (1 Cor. 15:44). At the present time, we have only the first fruits of the Spirit and are waiting for the full harvest, "the redemption of our body" (Rom. 8:23).

There is, however, a sense in which the Holy Spirit even now quickens our bodies. Jesus tells us in Matthew 12:28 that He cast out devils by the Spirit of God. We read in Acts 10:38, "How God anointed Jesus of Nazareth with the Holy Ghost and with power: who went about doing good, and healing all that were oppressed of the devil." In

James 5:14 the apostle writes, "Is any sick among you? let him call for the elders of the church; and let them pray over him, anointing him with oil in the name of the Lord." The oil in this passage (as elsewhere) is a type of the Holy Spirit, and the truth is set forth that the healing is the Holy Spirit's work.

God by His Holy Spirit does impart new health and vigor to these mortal bodies in the present life. To go to the extremes that many do and take the ground that the believer who is walking in fellowship with Christ need never be ill is to go farther than the Bible warrants us in going. It is true that the redemption of our bodies is secured by the atoning work of Christ, but until the Lord comes, we only enjoy the first fruits of that redemption.

We are waiting and sometimes groaning for our full place as sons manifested in the redemption of our bodies (Rom. 8:23). But while this is true, it is the clear teaching of Scripture, as well as a matter of personal experience on the part of thousands, that the life of the Holy Spirit does sweep through these bodies of ours in moments of weakness and of pain and sickness, imparting new health to them, delivering them from pain and filling them with abounding life. It is our privilege to know the quickening touch of the Holy Spirit in these bodies as well as in our minds and affections and will. It would be a great day for the church and for the glory of Jesus Christ if Christians would renounce forever all the devil's counterfeits of the Holy Spirit's work: Christian Science, mental healing, hypnotism, and the various other forms of occultism, and depend upon God by the power of His Holy Spirit to work in these bodies of ours what He in His unerring wisdom sees that we most need.

Chapter 20

The Baptism with the Holy Spirit

O ne of the most deeply significant phrases used in connection with the Holy Spirit in the Scriptures is "baptized with the Holy Ghost." John the Baptist was the first to use this phrase. In speaking of himself and the coming One he said,

> I indeed baptize you with water unto repentance: but he that cometh after me is mightier than I, whose shoes I am not worthy to bear: he shall baptize you with the Holy Ghost, and with fire. (Matt. 3:11)

The second "with" in this passage is in italics. It is not found in the Greek. There are not two different baptisms spoken of, the one with the Holy Ghost and one with fire, but one baptism with the Holy Wind and Fire. Jesus afterwards used the same expression. In Acts 1:5, He says, "For John truly baptized with water; but ye shall be baptized with the Holy Ghost not many days hence." When this promise of John the Baptist and of our Lord was fulfilled in Acts 2:3–4, we read, "And there appeared unto them cloven tongues like as of fire, and it sat upon each one of them. And they were all filled with the Holy Ghost." Here we have another expression, "filled with the Holy Ghost," used synonymously with "baptized with the Holy Spirit."

We read again in Acts,

While Peter yet spake these words, the Holy Ghost fell on all them which heard the word. And they of the circumcision which believed were astonished, as many as came with Peter, because that on the Gentiles also was poured out the gift of the Holy Ghost. For they heard them speak with tongues, and magnify God. (Acts 10:44–46)

Peter himself, afterwards describing this experience in Jerusalem, tells the story in this way:

And as I began to speak, the Holy Ghost fell on them, as on us at the beginning. Then remembered I the word of the Lord, how that he said, John indeed baptized with water; but ye shall be baptized with the Holy Ghost. Forasmuch then as God gave them the like gift as he did unto us, who believed on the Lord Jesus Christ; what was I, that I could withstand God? (Acts 11:15–17)

Here Peter distinctly calls the experience which came to Cornelius and his household, being "baptized with the Holy Ghost," so we see that the expressions "the Holy Ghost fell" and "the gift of the Holy Ghost" are practically synonymous expressions with "baptized with the Holy Ghost." Still other expressions are used to describe this blessing, such as "receive the Holy Ghost" (see Acts 2:38; 19:2–6); "the Holy Ghost came on them" (see Acts 19:2–6); "gift of the Holy Ghost" (see 1 Corinthians 12:4, 11, 13; Hebrews 2:4); "I send the promise of my Father upon you;" and "endued with power from on high" (Luke 24:49).

WHAT IS THE BAPTISM WITH THE HOLY SPIRIT?

In the first place the baptism with the Holy Spirit is a definite experience of which one may and ought to know whether he has received it or not.

This is evident from our Lord's command to His disciples in Luke 24:49 and in Acts 1:4 that they should not depart from Jerusalem to undertake the work which He had commissioned them to do until they had received this promise of the Father. It is also evident from Acts 8:15–16, where we are distinctly told, "the Holy Ghost...as yet was fallen upon none of them." It is evident also from Acts 19:2 (RV), where Paul put to the little group of disciples at Ephesus the definite question, "Did ye receive the Holy Ghost when ye believed?"

It is evident that the receiving of the Holy Ghost was an experience so definite that one could answer yes or no to the question whether they had received the Holy Spirit. In this case the disciples definitely answered, "Nay, we did not so much as hear whether the Holy Ghost was given" (Acts

19:2 RV). They did not say what our KJV makes them say, which is that they did not so much as hear whether there was any Holy Ghost. They knew that there was a Holy Ghost. They knew furthermore that there was a definite promise of the baptism with the Holy Ghost, but they had not heard that that promise had been as yet fulfilled. Paul told them that it had and took steps whereby they were definitely baptized with the Holy Spirit before that meeting closed.

It is equally evident from Galatians 3:2 that the baptism with the Holy Spirit is a definite experience of which one may know whether he has received it or not. In this passage Paul says to the believers in Galatia, "This only would I learn of you, Received ye the Spirit by the works of the law, or by the hearing of faith?" Their receiving the Spirit had been so definite as a matter of personal consciousness that Paul could appeal to it as a ground for his argument.

In our day there is much talk about the baptism with the Holy Spirit and prayer for the baptism with the Spirit that is altogether vague and indefinite. Men arise in meetings and pray that they may be baptized with the Holy Spirit. If you should go afterwards to the one who offered the prayer and put to him the question, "Did you receive what you asked? Were you baptized with the Holy Spirit?" it is quite likely that he would hesitate and falter and say, "I hope so." But, there is none of this indefiniteness in the Bible. The Bible is clear as day on this, as on every other point. It sets forth an experience so definite and so real that one may know whether or not he has received the baptism with the Holy Spirit and can answer yes or no to the question, "Have you received the Holy Ghost?"

In the second place it is evident that the baptism with the Holy Spirit is an operation of the Holy Spirit distinct from, and additional to, His regenerating work.

This is evident from Acts 1:5: "For John truly baptized with water; but ye shall be baptized with the Holy Ghost not many days hence." It is clear then that the disciples had not as yet been baptized with the Holy Ghost, that they were to be thus baptized not many days hence, but the men to whom Jesus spoke these words were already new men. They had been so pronounced by our Lord Himself. He had said to them in John 15:3, "Now ye are clean through the word which I have spoken unto you." What does "clean through the word" mean? The question is answered in 1 Peter 1:23: "Being born again, not of corruptible seed, but of incorruptible, by the word of God, which liveth and abideth forever."

A little earlier on the same night, Jesus had said to them in John 13:10, "He that is washed needeth not save to wash his feet, but is clean every whit: and ye are clean, but not all." The Lord Jesus had pronounced that apostolic company clean—reborn men—with the exception of the one who never was a reborn man, Judas Iscariot, who should betray Him. (See verse 11.) The remaining eleven Jesus Christ had pronounced reborn men. Yet He tells these same men in Acts 1:5 that the baptism with the Holy Spirit was an experience that they had not as yet realized, that still lay in the future. So it is evident that it is one thing to be born again by the Holy Spirit through the Word and something distinct from this and additional to it to be baptized with the Holy Spirit.

The same thing is evident from Acts 8:12, compared with the fifteenth and sixteenth verses of the same chapter. In the twelfth verse we read that a large company of disciples had believed the preaching of Philip concerning the kingdom of God and the name of Jesus Christ, and "were baptized in the name of the Lord Jesus" (Rom. 8:16). Certainly in this company of baptized believers there were at least some reborn people. Whatever the true form of water baptism may be, they undoubtedly had been baptized by it because the baptizing had been done by a Spirit-commissioned man, but we read,

> *When they* [that is, Peter and John] *were come down, prayed for them, that they might receive the Holy Ghost: (For as yet he was fallen upon none of them: only they were baptized in the name of the Lord Jesus.)*
> *(Rom. 8:15–16)*

Baptized believers they were; they had been baptized into the name of the Lord Jesus. Reborn men some of them most assuredly were, and yet not one of them as yet had received, or been baptized with, the Holy Ghost. So again, it is evident that the baptism with the Holy Spirit is an operation of the

Holy Spirit distinct from and additional to His regenerating work. A man may be reborn by the Holy Spirit and still not be baptized with the Holy Spirit. In being reborn, there is the impartation of life by the Spirit's power, and the one who receives it is saved. In the baptism with the Holy Spirit, there is the impartation of power, and the one who receives it is fitted for service.

The baptism with the Holy Spirit, however, may take place at the moment of rebirth. It did, for example, in the household of Cornelius. We read in Acts 10:43 that, while Peter was preaching, he came to the point where he said concerning Jesus, "To him give all the prophets witness, that through his name whosoever believeth in him shall receive remission of sins." At that point Cornelius and his household believed, and we immediately read,

> *While Peter yet spake these words, the Holy Ghost fell on all them which heard the word. And they of the circumcision which believed were astonished, as many as came with Peter, because that on the Gentiles also was poured out the gift of the Holy Ghost.*
> *(Acts 10:44–45)*

The moment they believed the testimony about Jesus, they were baptized with the Holy Ghost, even before they were baptized with water. Rebirth and the baptism with the Holy Spirit took place practically at the same moment, and so they do in many an experience today. It would seem as if, in a normal condition of the church, this would be the usual experience. But the church is not in a normal condition today. A very large part of the church is in the place where the believers in Samaria were before Peter and John came and where the disciples in Ephesus were before Paul came and told them of their larger privilege—baptized believers, baptized into the name of the Lord Jesus, baptized unto repentance and remission of sins, but not as yet baptized with the Holy Ghost. Nevertheless, the baptism with the Holy Spirit is the birthright of every believer. It was purchased for us by the atoning death of Christ. When He ascended to the right hand of the Father, He received the promise of the Father and shed Him forth upon the church, and if anyone today has not the baptism with the Holy Spirit as a personal experience, it is because he has not claimed his birthright.

Potentially, every member of the body of Christ is baptized with the Holy Spirit: "For by one Spirit are we all baptized into one body, whether we be Jews or Gentiles, whether we be bond or free; and have been all made to drink into one Spirit" (1 Cor. 12:13). But there are many believers with whom that which is potentially theirs has not become a matter of real, actual, personal experience. All men are potentially justified in the atoning death of Jesus Christ on the cross; that is, justification is provided for them and belongs to them. (See Romans 5:18.) What potentially belongs to every man, each man must appropriate to himself by faith in Christ. Then justification is actually and experientially his; just so, while the baptism with the Holy Spirit is potentially the possession of every believer, each individual believer must appropriate it for himself before it is experientially his. We may go still further than this and say that it is only by the baptism with the Holy Spirit that one becomes in the fullest sense a member of the body of Christ because it is only by the baptism with the Spirit that he receives power to perform those functions for which God has appointed him as a part of the body.

As we have already seen every true believer has the Holy Spirit (see Romans 8:9), but not every believer has the baptism with the Holy Spirit (though every believer may have, as we have just seen). It is one thing to have the Holy Spirit dwell within us, perhaps dwelling within us way back in some hidden sanctuary of our being, back of definite consciousness, and something far different, something vastly more, to have the Holy Spirit take complete possession of the one whom He inhabits. There are those who press the fact that every believer potentially has the baptism with the Spirit to such an extent that they clearly teach that every believer has the baptism with the Spirit as an actual experience. But unless the baptism with the Spirit today is something radically different from what the baptism with the Spirit was in the early church, indeed unless it is something not at all real, then either a very large proportion of those whom we ordinarily consider believers are not believers or else one may be a believer and a reborn man without having been baptized with the Holy Spirit. Certainly, the latter was the case in the early church. It was the case with the apostles before Pentecost; it was the case with the church in Ephesus; it was the case with the church in Samaria. And there are thousands today who can testify to having received Christ and been born again, and then afterwards, sometimes long afterwards, having been baptized with the Holy Ghost as a definite experience.

This is a matter of great practical importance. There are many who are not enjoying the fullness of privilege that they might enjoy because by pushing individual verses in the Scriptures beyond what they will bear and against the plain teaching of the Scriptures as a whole, they are trying to persuade themselves that they have already been baptized with the Holy Spirit when they have not. If they would only admit to themselves that they had not, they could then take the steps whereby they would be baptized with the Holy Spirit as a matter of definite, personal experience.

The next thing which is clear from the teaching of Scripture is that the baptism with the Holy Spirit is always connected with and primarily for the purpose of testimony and service.

Our Lord in speaking of this baptism which they were so soon to receive said in Luke 24:49: "And, behold I send the promise of My Father upon you: but tarry ye in the city of Jerusalem, until ye be endued with power from on high." And again He said,

> *For John truly baptized with water; but ye shall be baptized with the Holy Ghost not*

many days hence...But ye shall receive
power, after that the Holy Ghost is come
upon you: and ye shall be witnesses unto me,
both in Jerusalem, and in all Judaea, and
in Samaria, and unto the uttermost part of
the earth. (Acts 1:5, 8)

In the record of the fulfillment of this promise
of our Lord, we read, "And they were all filled with
the Holy Ghost, and began to speak with other
tongues, as the Spirit gave them utterance" (Acts
2:4). Then follows the detailed account of what Peter said and of the result. The result was that Peter and the other apostles spoke with such power
that three thousand people that day were convicted of sin, had renounced their sin, had confessed their acceptance of Jesus Christ in baptism,
and had continued steadfastly in the apostles' doctrine and fellowship and in the breaking of bread
and in prayer ever afterwards. (See Acts 2:41–42.)

In Acts 4:31–33, we read that when the apostles on another occasion were filled with the Holy
Spirit, the result was that they "spake the word of
God with boldness" and that "with great power
gave the apostles witness of the resurrection of the
Lord Jesus." The following is a description of Paul
being baptized with the Holy Spirit:

And Ananias went his way, and entered into
the house; and putting his hands on him
said, Brother Saul, the Lord, even Jesus,
that appeared unto thee in the way as thou
camest, hath sent me, that thou mightest re-
ceive thy sight, and be filled with the Holy

Ghost. And immediately there fell from his eyes as it had been scales: and he received sight forthwith, and arose, and was baptized. And when he had received meat, he was strengthened...And straightway he preached Christ in the synagogues, that he is the Son of God. (Acts 9:17–20)

And in the twenty-second verse we read that he "confounded the Jews which dwelt at Damascus, proving that this is very Christ."

In 1 Corinthians chapter twelve we have the fullest discussion of the baptism with the Holy Spirit found in any passage in the Bible. This is the classical passage on the whole subject. The results there recorded are gifts for service. The baptism with the Holy Spirit is not primarily intended to make believers happy but to make them useful. It is not intended merely for the ecstasy of the individual believer; it is intended primarily for his efficiency in service. I do not say that the baptism with the Holy Spirit will not make the believer happy for part of the fruit of the Spirit is "joy." If one is baptized with the Holy Spirit, joy must inevitably result. I have never known one to be baptized with the Holy Spirit into whose life there did not come, sooner or later, a new joy, a higher and purer and fuller joy than he had ever known before.

But this is not the prime purpose of the baptism nor the most important and prominent result. Great emphasis needs to be laid upon this point, for there are many Christians who, in seeking the baptism with the Spirit, are seeking personal ecstasy and rapture. They go to conventions and conferences for the deepening of the Christian life and come back and tell what a wonderful blessing they have received, referring to some new ecstasy that has come into their hearts. However, when you watch them, it is difficult to see that they are any more useful to their pastors or their churches than they were before, and one is compelled to think that whatever they have received, they have not received the real baptism with the Holy Spirit.

Ecstasies and raptures are all right in their places. When they come, thank God for them—I know something about them—but in a world such as we live in today, where sin and self-righteousness and unbelief are so triumphant, where there is such an awful tide of men, women, and young people sweeping on towards eternal perdition, I would rather go through my whole life and never have one touch of ecstasy but have power to witness for Christ. I would rather have power to win others for Christ and thus to save them than to have raptures 365 days in the year but have no power to stem the awful tide of sin and bring men, women, and children to a saving knowledge of my Lord and Savior, Jesus Christ.

The purpose of the baptism with the Holy Spirit is not primarily to make believers individually holy. I do not say that it is not the work of the Holy Spirit to make believers holy, for as we have already seen, He is the Spirit of Holiness, and the only way we shall ever attain holiness is by His power. I do not even say that the baptism with the Holy Spirit will not result in a great spiritual transformation and uplift and cleansing, for the promise is, "He shall baptize you with the Holy Ghost, and with fire" (Matt. 3:11). The thought of fire as used in this connection is the thought of searching, refining, cleansing, and consuming. A wonderful transformation took place in the apostles at Pentecost and has taken place in thousands who have been baptized with the Holy Spirit since Pentecost, but the primary purpose of the baptism with the Holy Spirit is efficiency in testimony and service. It has to do more with gifts for service than with graces of character. It is the impartation of spiritual power or gifts in service, and sometimes one may have rare gifts by the Spirit's power and yet manifest few of the graces of the Spirit. (See 1 Corinthians 13:1–3 and Matthew 7:22–23.) In every passage in the Bible in which the baptism with the Holy Spirit is mentioned, it is connected with testimony or service.

Chapter 21

The Results of the Baptism with the Holy Spirit

We shall perhaps get a clearer idea of just what the baptism with the Holy Spirit is if we stop to consider what the results are of the baptism with the Holy Spirit.

The specific manifestations of the baptism with the Holy Spirit are not precisely the same in all people.

This appears very clearly in 1 Corinthians:

Now there are diversities of gifts, but the same Spirit. And there are differences of administrations, but the same Lord. And there are diversities of operations, but it is the same God which worketh all in all. But the manifestation of the Spirit is given to every man to profit withal. For to one is given by the Spirit the word of wisdom; to another the word of knowledge by the same Spirit; To another faith by the same Spirit; to another the gifts of healing by the same Spirit; To another the working of miracles;

*to another prophecy; to another discerning of
spirits; to another divers kinds of tongues; to
another the interpretation of tongues: But all
these worketh that one and the selfsame
Spirit, dividing to every man severally as he
will. For as the body is one, and hath many
members, and all the members of that one
body, being many, are one body: so also is
Christ. For by one Spirit are we all baptized
into one body, whether we be Jews or Gentiles, whether we be bond or free; and have
been all made to drink into one Spirit.*

(1 Cor. 12:4–13)

Here we see one baptism but a great variety of
manifestations of the power of that baptism. There
are diversities of gifts but the same Spirit. The
gifts vary with the different areas of service to
which God calls different people. The church is a
body, and different members of the body have different functions. The Spirit imparts to the one
who is baptized with the Spirit those gifts which fit
him for the service to which God has called him. It
is very important to bear this in mind. Through
the failure to see this, many have gone entirely
astray on the whole subject.

In my early study of the subject, I noticed the
fact that in many instances those who were baptized with the Holy Spirit spoke with tongues (for
example, see Acts 2:4; 10:46; 19:6), and I wondered
if everyone who was baptized with the Holy Spirit
would speak with tongues. I did not know of anyone who was speaking with tongues today, and so I
wondered still further whether the baptism with

the Holy Spirit was for the present age. But one day I was studying 1 Corinthians chapter twelve and noticed what Paul said to the believers in that wonderfully gifted church in Corinth, all of whom had been pronounced to be baptized with the Spirit (see v. 13):

> *And God hath set some in the church, first apostles, secondarily prophets, thirdly teachers, after that miracles, then gifts of healings, helps, governments, diversities of tongues. Are all apostles? are all prophets? are all teachers? are all workers of miracles? Have all the gift of healing? do all speak with tongues? do all interpret?*
>
> *(1 Cor. 12:28–30)*

So I saw it was clearly taught in the Scriptures that one might be baptized with the Holy Spirit and still not have the gift of tongues. I saw furthermore that the gift of tongues, according to the Scripture, was the last and the least important of all the gifts and that we were urged to desire earnestly the greater gifts. (See 1 Corinthians 12:31; 14:5, 12, 14, 18, 19, 27, 28.)

A little later I was tempted to fall into another error, more specious but in reality just as unscriptural as this, namely, that if one were baptized with the Holy Spirit, he would receive the gift relating to an evangelist. I had read the story of D. L. Moody, of Charles G. Finney, and of others who were baptized with the Holy Spirit and of the power that came to them as evangelists. The thought was suggested that if anyone is baptized with the Holy Spirit, he should also obtain power as an evangelist. This was also unscriptural. If God has called a man to be an evangelist and is baptized with the Holy Spirit, he will receive power as an evangelist, but if God has called him to be something else, he will receive power to become something else. Three great evils come from the error of thinking that everyone who is baptized with the Holy Spirit will receive power as an evangelist.

The first evil is the evil of disappointment. There are many who seek the baptism with the Holy Spirit expecting power as an evangelist, but God has not called them to that work. Though they really meet the conditions of receiving the baptism with the Spirit and do receive the baptism with the Spirit, power as an evangelist does not come. In many cases this results in bitter disappointment and sometimes even in despair. The one who has expected the power of an evangelist and has not received it sometimes even questions whether he is a child of God. If he had properly understood the matter, he would have known that the fact that he had not received power as an evangelist is no proof that he has not received the baptism with the Spirit, and much less is it a proof that he is not a child of God.

This second evil is graver still, namely, the evil of presumption. A man whom God has not called to the work of an evangelist or a minister oftentimes rushes into it because he has received, or imagines he has received, the baptism with the Holy Spirit. He thinks all a man needs to become a preacher is the baptism with the Holy Spirit. This is not true. In order to succeed as a minister, a man needs a call to that specific work, and furthermore, he needs the knowledge of God's Word that will prepare him for the work. If a man is called to the ministry and studies the Word until he has something to preach, if then he is baptized with the Holy Spirit, he will have success as a preacher. But if he is not called to that work, or if he has not the knowledge of the Word of God that is necessary, he will not succeed in the work even though he receives the baptism with the Holy Spirit.

The third evil is greater still, namely, the evil of indifference. There are many who know that they are not called to the work of preaching. If then they think that the baptism with the Holy Spirit simply imparts power as an evangelist, or power to preach, the matter of the baptism with the Holy Spirit is one of no personal concern to them. For example, consider a mother with a large family of children. She knows perfectly well, or at least it is hoped that she knows, that she is not called to do the work of an evangelist. She knows that her duty lies with her children and her home. If she reads or hears about the baptism with the Holy Spirit and gets the impression that the baptism with the Holy Spirit simply imparts power to do the work of an evangelist or to preach, she will think, "the evangelist needs this blessing, my minister needs this blessing, but it is not for me." But if she understands the matter as it is taught in the Bible, that, while the baptism with the Spirit imparts power, the way in which the power will be manifested depends entirely upon the area of work to which God calls us; if she understands that no efficient work can be done without it and sees still further that there is no function in the church of Jesus Christ today more holy and sacred than that of sanctified motherhood, she will say, "The evangelist may need this baptism, my minister may need this baptism, but I must have it to bring up my children in the nurture and admonition of the Lord."

While there are diversities of gifts and manifestations of the baptism with the Holy Spirit, there will be some gift to everyone thus baptized.

We read in 1 Corinthians 12:7, "But the manifestation of the Spirit is given to every man to profit withal." Each most insignificant member of the body of Christ has some function to perform in that body. The body grows by that "which every joint supplieth" (Eph. 4:16), and to each least significant joint, the Holy Spirit imparts power to perform the function that belongs to him.

The Holy Spirit decides how the baptism with the Spirit will manifest itself in any given case.

We read in 1 Corinthians 12:11, "But all these worketh that one and the selfsame Spirit, dividing to every man severally as he will." The Holy Spirit is absolutely sovereign in deciding how—that is, in what special gift, operation, or power—the baptism with the Holy Spirit will manifest itself. It is not for us to pick out some field of service and then ask the Holy Spirit to qualify us for that service. It is not for us to select some gift and then ask the Holy Spirit to impart to us this self-chosen gift. It is for us to simply put ourselves entirely at the disposal of the Holy Spirit to send us where He will, to select for us what kind of service He will, and to impart to us what gifts He will. He is absolutely sovereign and our position is that of unconditional surrender to Him. I am glad that this is so. I rejoice that He, in His infinite wisdom and love, is to select the field of service and the gifts, and that this is not to be left to me in my short-sightedness and folly. It is because of the failure to recognize this absolute sovereignty of the Spirit that many fail to obtain the blessing and meet with disappointment. They are trying to select their own gift and so get none.

I once knew an earnest child of God in Scotland who, hearing of the baptism with the Holy Spirit and the power that resulted from it, gave up at a great sacrifice his work as a ship plater for which he was receiving large wages. He heard that there was a great need of ministers in the Northwest in America. He came to the Northwest. He met the conditions of the baptism with the Holy Spirit, and I believe he was really baptized with the Holy Spirit. But God had not chosen him for the work of an evangelist, and the power as an evangelist did not come to him. No field seemed to open, and he was in great despondency. He even questioned his acceptance before God. One

morning he came into our church in Minneapolis
and heard me speak upon the baptism with the
Holy Spirit. As I pointed out that the baptism with
the Holy Spirit manifested itself in many different
ways and the fact that one did not have power as
an evangelist was no proof that he had not received the baptism with the Holy Spirit, light came
into his heart. He put himself unreservedly into
God's hands for Him to choose the field of labor
and the gifts. An opening soon came to him as a
Sunday school missionary. Then, when he had
given up choosing for himself and left it with the
Holy Spirit to divide to him as He would, a strange
thing happened; he did receive power as an evangelist and went through the country districts in
one of our northwestern states with mighty power
as an evangelist.

**While the power may be of one kind in one person and of
another kind in another person, there will always be
power, the very power of God, when one is baptized with
the Holy Spirit.**

> *For John truly baptized with water; but ye
> shall be baptized with the Holy Ghost not
> many days hence...But ye shall receive
> power, after that the Holy Ghost is come
> upon you: and ye shall be witnesses unto me
> both in Jerusalem, and in all Judaea, and
> in Samaria, and unto the uttermost part of
> the earth. (Acts 1:5–8)*

As truly as anyone who reads these pages,
who has not already received the baptism with the

Holy Spirit, seeks it in God's way, he will obtain it. Then, there will come into his service a power that was never there before, power for the very work to which God has called him. This is not only the teaching of Scripture; it is the teaching of religious experience throughout the centuries. Religious biographies abound in instances of men who have worked as best they could until one day they were led to see that there was such an experience as the baptism with the Holy Spirit and to seek it and obtain it. From that hour, there came into their service a new power that utterly transformed its character.

In this matter, one thinks first of such men as Finney and Moody and Brainerd, but cases of this nature are not confined to a few exceptional men. They are common. I have personally met and corresponded with hundreds and thousands of people around the globe who could testify definitely to the new power that God has granted them through the baptism with the Holy Spirit. These thousands of men and women were in all branches of Christian service; some of them are ministers of the Gospel, some evangelists, some mission workers, some YMCA secretaries, Sunday-school teachers, fathers, mothers, personal workers, etc. Nothing could possibly exceed the clearness and the confidence and the joyfulness of many of these testimonies.

I will not soon forget a minister whom I met some years ago at a State Convention of the Young People's Society of Christian Endeavor at New Britain, Connecticut. I was speaking upon the subject of personal work, and as I drew the address to a close, I said that in order to do effective personal work, we must be baptized with the Holy Spirit. In a very few sentences I explained what I meant by that.

At the close of the address, this minister came to me on the platform and said, "I do not have this blessing you have been speaking about, but I want it. Will you pray for me?"

I said, "Why not pray right now?"

He said, "I will."

We put two chairs side by side and turned our backs upon the crowd as they passed out of the armory. He prayed and I prayed that he might be baptized with the Holy Spirit. Then we separated. Some weeks after that, one who had witnessed the scene came to me at a convention in Washington and told me how this minister had gone back to his church a transformed man, that now his congregations filled the church, that it was largely composed of young men, and that there were conversions at every service. Some years after that, this minister was called to another field of service. His most spiritually minded friends advised him not to go because all the ruling elements in the church to which he had been called were against aggressive evangelistic work, but for some reason or other, he felt it was the call of God and accepted it. In six months, there were sixty-nine conversions, and thirty-eight of them were businessmen of the town.

After attending an Interprovincial Convention of the Young Men's Christian Association (YMCA) of the Provinces of Canada in Montreal some years ago, I received a letter from a young man. He wrote, "I was present at your last meeting in Montreal. I heard you speak upon the baptism with the Holy Spirit. I went to my room and sought that baptism for myself and received it. I am chairman of the Lookout Committee of the Christian Endeavor Society of our church. I called together the other members of the committee. I found that two of them had been at the meeting and had already been baptized with the Holy Spirit. Then we prayed for the other members of the committee, and they were baptized with the Holy Spirit. Now we are going out into the church, and the young people of the church are being brought to Christ right along."

A lady and gentleman once came to me at a convention and told me how, though they had never seen me before, they had read the report of an address on the baptism with the Holy Spirit delivered in Boston at a Christian workers' convention and that they had sought this baptism and had received it. The man then told me the blessing that had come into his service as superintendent of the Sunday school. When he had finished, his wife broke in and said, "Yes, and the best part of it is, I have been able to get into the hearts of my own children, which I was never able to do before."

Here were three distinctly different areas of service, but there was power in each case. The results of that power may not, however, be manifest at once in conversions. Stephen was filled with the Holy Spirit, but as he witnessed in the power of the Holy Spirit for his risen Lord, he saw no conversions at the time. All he saw was the gnashing of teeth, the angry looks, and the merciless rocks, and so it may be with us. However, there was a conversion, even in that case, though it was a long time before it was seen, and that conversion, the conversion of Saul of Tarsus, was worth more than hundreds of ordinary conversions.

Another result of the baptism with the Holy Spirit will be boldness in testimony and service.

We read in Acts 4:31, "And when they had prayed, the place was shaken where they were assembled together; and they were all filled with the Holy Ghost, and they spake the word of God with boldness." The baptism with the Holy Spirit imparts to those who receive it new liberty and fearlessness in testimony for Christ. It converts cowards into heroes.

Upon the night of our Lord's crucifixion, Peter proved himself a craven coward. He denied with oaths and curses that he knew the Lord. But after Pentecost, this same Peter was brought before the very council that had condemned Jesus to death, and he himself was threatened. However, filled with the Holy Ghost, he said,

> *Ye rulers of the people, and elders of Israel,*
> *If we this day be examined of the good deed*
> *done to the impotent man, by what means he*
> *is made whole; Be it known unto you all,*
> *and to all the people of Israel, that by the*
> *name of Jesus Christ of Nazareth, whom ye*

*crucified, whom God raised from the dead,
even by him doth this man stand here before
you whole. This is the stone which was set at
nought of you builders, which is become the
head of the corner. Neither is there salvation
in any other: for there is none other name
under heaven given among men, whereby we
must be saved.* (Acts 4:8–12)

A little later when the council commanded
him and his companion, John, not to speak or
teach in the name of Jesus, they answered,
"Whether it be right in the sight of God to hearken
unto you more than unto God, judge ye. For we
cannot but speak the things which we have seen
and heard" (Acts 4:19–20). On a still later occasion, when they were threatened and commanded
not to speak and when their lives were in jeopardy,
Peter told the council to their faces,

*We ought to obey God rather than men. The
God of our fathers raised up Jesus, whom ye
slew and hanged on a tree. Him hath God
exalted with his right hand to be a Prince
and a Saviour, for to give repentance to Israel, and forgiveness of sins. And we are his
witnesses of these things; and so is also the
Holy Ghost, whom God hath given to them
that obey Him.* (Acts 5:29–32)

The natural timidity of many a man today
vanishes when he is filled with the Holy Spirit.
With great boldness and liberty, with utter fearlessness of consequences, he gives his testimony
for Jesus Christ.

The baptism with the Holy Spirit causes the one who receives it to be occupied with God and Christ and spiritual things.

In the record of the day of Pentecost, we read,

They were all filled with the Holy Ghost, and began to speak with other tongues, as the Spirit gave them utterance...And they were all amazed and marvelled, saying one to another, Behold, are not all these which speak Galilaeans? And how hear we every man in our own tongue, wherein we were born...Cretes and Arabians, we do hear them speak in our tongues the wonderful works of God. (Acts 2:4–11)

Then follows Peter's sermon, a sermon that from start to finish is entirely taken up with Jesus Christ and His glory:

Then Peter, filled with the Holy Ghost, said unto them, Ye rulers of the people, and elders of Israel, If we this day be examined of the good deed done to the impotent man, by what means he is made whole; Be it known unto you all, and to all the people of Israel, that by the name of Jesus Christ of Nazareth, whom ye crucified, whom God raised from the dead, even by him doth this man stand here before you whole. (Acts 4:8–10)

On a later day we read,

And when they had prayed, the place was shaken where they were assembled together;

and they were all filled with the Holy Ghost,
and they spake the word of God with bold-
ness...And with great power gave the apos-
tles witness of the resurrection of the Lord
Jesus: and great grace was upon them all
(Acts 4:31–33)

We read of Saul of Tarsus, that when he had been filled with the Holy Spirit, "straightway in the synagogues he proclaimed Jesus" (Acts 4:20 RV). We read of the household of Cornelius:

While Peter yet spake these words, the Holy
Ghost fell on all them which heard the word.
And they of the circumcision which believed
were astonished, as many as came with Pe-
ter, because that on the Gentiles also was
poured out the gift of the Holy Ghost. For
they heard them speak with tongues, and
magnify God.   (Acts 10:44–46)

Here we see the whole household of Cornelius, as soon as they were filled with the Holy Spirit, magnifying God.

In Ephesians 5:18–19, we are told that the result of being filled with the Spirit is that those who are thus filled will speak to one another in psalms and hymns and spiritual songs, singing and making melody in their hearts to the Lord. Men who are filled with the Holy Spirit will not be singing sentimental ballads, not comic ditties, nor operatic airs while the power of the Holy Ghost is upon them. If the Holy Ghost should come upon anyone while listening to one of the most innocent of the world's songs, he would not enjoy it and would long to hear something about Christ. Men who are baptized with the Holy Spirit do not talk much about self but much about God and especially much about Christ. This is necessarily so, as it is the Holy Spirit's office to bear witness to the glorified Christ. (See John 15:26; 16:14.)

To sum up everything that has been said about the results of the baptism with the Holy Spirit: the baptism with the Holy Spirit is the Spirit of God coming upon the believer, filling his mind with a real apprehension of truth, especially of Christ, taking possession of his faculties, and imparting to him gifts not otherwise his but which qualify him for the service to which God has called him.

Chapter 22

The Necessity of the Baptism with the Holy Spirit

The New Testament has much to say about the necessity for the baptism with the Holy Spirit. When our Lord was about to leave His disciples to go to be with the Father, He said, "And, behold, I send the promise of my Father upon you: but tarry ye in the city of Jerusalem, until ye be endued with power from on high" (Luke 24:49). He had just commissioned them to be His witnesses to all nations, beginning at Jerusalem (see vv. 47–48), but He tells them here that before they undertake this witnessing, they must wait until they receive the promise of the Father. They were thus endued with power from on high for the work of witnessing which they were to undertake. There is no doubt as to what Jesus meant by "the promise of my Father," for which they were to wait before beginning the ministry that He had laid upon them, for in Acts we read,

And, being assembled together with them, [He] commanded them that they should not

depart from Jerusalem, but wait for the promise of the Father, which, saith he, ye have heard of me. For John truly baptized with water; but ye shall be baptized with the Holy Ghost not many days hence. (Acts 1:4–5)

It is evident then that "the promise of the Father" through which the endowment of power was to come was the baptism with the Holy Spirit. He went on to tell His disciples,

Ye shall receive power, after that the Holy Ghost is come upon you: and ye shall be witnesses unto me both in Jerusalem, and in all Judaea, and in Samaria, and unto the uttermost part of the earth. (Acts 1:8)

Now who were the men to whom Jesus said this? The men were the disciples whom He Himself had trained for the work. For more than three years, they had lived in the closest intimacy with Him; they had been eyewitnesses of His miracles, of His death, of His resurrection, and in a few moments were to be eyewitnesses of His ascension as He was taken up right before their eyes into heaven. And what were they to do? Simply go and tell the world what their own eyes had seen and what their own ears had heard from the lips of the Son of God. Were they not equipped for the work? With our modern ideas of preparation for Christian work, we should say that they were thoroughly equipped. But Jesus said, "No, you are not equipped. There is another preparation in addition to the preparation already received, so absolutely necessary for effective work that you must not stir one step until you receive it. This other preparation is the promise of the Father, the baptism with the Holy Spirit." If the apostles with their altogether exceptional fitting for the work which they were to undertake needed this preparation for work, how much more do we?

In the light of what Jesus required of His disciples before undertaking the work, does it not seem like the most daring presumption for any of us to undertake to witness and work for Christ until we also have received the promise of the Father, the baptism with the Holy Spirit? There was apparently imperative need that something be done at once. The whole world was perishing, and they alone knew the saving truth. Nevertheless, Jesus strictly charged them to "wait." Could there be a stronger testimony to the absolute necessity and importance of the baptism with the Holy Spirit as a preparation for work that should be acceptable to Christ?

But this is not all. In Acts 10:38 we read, "How God anointed Jesus of Nazareth with the Holy Ghost and with power: who went about doing good, and healing all that were oppressed of the devil; for God was with him." To what does this refer in the recorded life of Jesus Christ? If we will turn to Luke 3:21–22, and Luke 4:1, 4, 17–18 we will get our answer. In Luke 3:21–22, we read that after Jesus had been baptized and was praying, "The heaven was opened, and the Holy Ghost descended in a bodily shape like a dove upon him, and a voice came from heaven, which said, Thou art my beloved Son; in thee I am well pleased."

Then the next thing that we read, with nothing intervening but the human genealogy of Jesus, is the following: "And Jesus being full of the Holy Ghost returned from Jordan, and was led by the Spirit into the wilderness" (Luke 4:1). Then follows the story of His temptation. Then we read, "And Jesus returned in the power of the Spirit into Galilee: and there went out a fame of him through all the region round about" (Luke 4:14). Further, we read,

> And there was delivered unto him the book of the prophet Esaias [Isaiah]. And when he had opened the book, he found the place where it was written, The Spirit of the Lord is upon me, because he hath anointed me to preach...."
> (Luke 4:17–18)

Evidently then, it was at the Jordan, in connection with His baptism, that Jesus was anointed with the Holy Spirit and power, and He did not enter upon His public ministry until He was thus baptized with the Holy Spirit. And who was Jesus? It is the common belief of Christendom that He had been supernaturally conceived through the Holy Spirit's power, that He was the only begotten Son of God, that He was divine, very God of very God, and yet truly man. If such a One, "leaving us an example, that ye should follow his steps" (1 Pet. 2:21), did not venture upon His ministry for which the Father had sent Him until he was definitely baptized with the Holy Spirit, what is it for us to dare to do it? If in the light of these recorded facts we dare to do it, does it not seem like the

218

most unpardonable presumption? Doubtless it has been done in ignorance by many of us, but can we plead ignorance any longer?

It is evident that the baptism with the Holy Spirit is an absolutely necessary preparation for effective work for Christ along every line of service. We may have a very clear call to service, as clear it may be as the apostles had, but the charge is laid upon us as upon them, that before we begin that service we must tarry until we are clothed with power from on high. This endowment of power is through the baptism with the Holy Spirit.

Even yet, this is not all. We read in Acts 8:14–16:

> *Now when the apostles which were at Jerusalem heard that Samaria had received the word of God, they sent unto them Peter and John: Who, when they were come down, prayed for them, that they might receive the Holy Ghost (For as yet he was fallen upon none of them: only they were baptized in the name of the Lord Jesus).*

There was a great company of happy converts in Samaria, but when Peter and John came down to inspect the work, they evidently felt that there was something so essential that these young disciples had not received that before they did anything else, they must see to it that they received it.

In a similar way we read,

> *And it came to pass, that, while Apollos was at Corinth, Paul having passed through the*

*upper coasts came to Ephesus: and finding
certain disciples, He said unto them, Have
ye received the Holy Ghost since ye believed?*
(Acts 19:1–2)

When he found that they had not received the
Holy Spirit, the first thing that he saw to was that
they should receive the Holy Spirit. He did not go
on with the work with the outsiders until that little group of twelve disciples had been equipped for
service. So we see that when the apostles found
believers in Christ, the first thing that they always
did was to demand whether they had received the
Holy Spirit as a definite experience, and if not,
they saw to it at once that the steps were taken
whereby they should receive the Holy Spirit.

It is evident then that the baptism with the
Holy Spirit is absolutely necessary in every Christian for the service that Christ demands and expects of him. There are certainly few greater
mistakes that we are making today in our various
Christian enterprises than that of appointing men
to teach Sunday-school classes and do personal
work and even to preach the Gospel because they
have been converted and received a certain
amount of education, including perhaps a college
and seminary course, but have not as yet been
baptized with the Holy Spirit. We think that if a
man is hopefully pious and has had a college and
seminary education and comes out of it reasonably
orthodox, he is now ready for our hands to be laid
upon him and to be ordained to preach the Gospel.
But Jesus Christ says, "No." There is another

preparation so essential that a man must not undertake this work until he has received it. "Tarry ye [literally 'sit ye down']...until ye be endued with power from on high" (Luke 24:49).

A distinguished theological professor has said that the question, "Have you met God?" ought to be put to every candidate for the ministry. Yes, but we ought to go farther than this and be even more definite. To every candidate for the ministry we should put the question, "Have you been baptized with the Holy Spirit?" and if not, we should say to him as Jesus said to the first preachers of the Gospel, "Sit down until you are endued with power from on high."

Not only is this true of ordained ministers, it is true of every Christian, for all Christians are called to ministry of some kind. Any man who is in Christian work who has not received the baptism with the Holy Spirit ought to stop his work right where he is and not go on with it until he has been "endued with power from on high" (Luke 24:49).

What will our work do while we are waiting? The question can be answered by asking another, "What did the world do during these ten days while the early disciples were waiting?" They knew the saving truth, they alone knew it, yet in obedience to the Lord's command they were silent. The world was no loser. Beyond a doubt, when the power came, they accomplished more in one day than they would have accomplished in years if they had gone on in self-confident defiance and disobedience to Christ's command.

We, too, after we have received the baptism with the Spirit, will accomplish more real work for our Lord in one day than we ever would in years without this power. Even if it were necessary to spend days in waiting, they would be well spent, but we will see later that there is no need that we spend days in waiting, that the baptism with the Holy Spirit may be received today.

Someone may say that the apostles had gone on missionary tours during Christ's lifetime, even before they were baptized with the Holy Spirit. This is true, but that was before the Holy Spirit was given and before the command was given, "Tarry ye...until ye be endued with power from on high" (Luke 24:49). After that, it would have been disobedience and folly and presumption to have gone forth without this endowment, and we are living today after the Holy Spirit has been given and after the charge has been given to tarry until clothed.

Who can be baptized with the Holy Spirit?

We come now to the question of first importance, namely, who can be baptized with the Holy Spirit? At a convention some years ago, a very intelligent Christian woman, a well-known worker in educational as well as Sunday-school work, sent me this question, "You have told us of the necessity of the baptism with the Holy Spirit, but who can have this baptism? The church to which I belong teaches that the baptism with the Holy Spirit was confined to the apostolic age. Will you not tell us who can have the baptism with the Holy Spirit?" Fortunately, this question is answered in the most explicit terms in the Bible:

> *Then Peter said unto them, Repent, and be baptized every one of you in the name of Jesus Christ for the remission of sins, and ye shall receive the gift of the Holy Ghost. For the promise is unto you, and to your children, and to all that are afar off, even as many as the Lord our God shall call.*
>
> *(Acts 2:38–39)*

What is the promise to which Peter refers in the thirty-ninth verse? There are two interpretations of the passage: one is that the promise of this verse is the promise of salvation; the other is that the promise of this verse is the promise of the gift of the Holy Spirit (or the baptism with the Holy Spirit—a comparison of Scripture passages will show that the two expressions are synonymous).

Which is the correct interpretation? There are two laws of interpretation universally recognized among Bible scholars. These two laws are the law of usage (or *usus loquendi,* as it is called) and the law of context. Many a verse in the Bible standing alone might have two or three or even more possible interpretations, but when these two laws of interpretation are applied, it is settled to a certainty that only one of the various possible interpretations is the true interpretation.

The law of usage is this: when you find a word or phrase in any passage of Scripture and you wish to know what it means, do not go to a dictionary, but go to the Bible itself. Look up the various passages in which the word is used and especially how the particular writer being studied uses it and especially how it is used in that particular book in which the passage is found. Thus, you can determine what the precise meaning of the word or phrase is in the passage in question.

The law of context is this: when you study a passage, you should not take it out of its context but should look at what goes before it and what comes after it. While it might mean various things if it stood alone, it can only mean one thing in the context in which it is found.

Now let us apply these two laws to the passage in question. First of all, let us apply the law of usage. We are trying to discover what the expression "the promise" means in Acts 2:39. Turning back to Acts 1:4–5, we read,

> [He] *commanded them that they should not depart from Jerusalem, but wait for the promise of the Father, which, saith he, ye have heard of me. For John truly baptized with water; but ye shall be baptized with the Holy Ghost not many days hence.*

It is evident, then, that here the promise of the Father means the baptism with the Holy Spirit.

Turn now to Acts 2:33: "Therefore being by the right hand of God exalted, and having received of the Father the promise of the Holy Ghost, he hath shed forth this, which ye now see and hear." In this passage we are told in so many words that the promise is the promise of the Holy Spirit. If this peculiar expression means the baptism with the Holy Spirit in Acts 1:4–5, and the same thing in Acts 2:33, by what same law of interpretation can it possibly mean something entirely different six verses farther down in Acts 2:39? So the law of usage establishes it that the promise of Acts 2:39 is the promise of the baptism with the Holy Spirit.

Now let us apply the law of context, and we will find that, if possible, this is even more decisive. Read the following verses:

> *Then Peter said unto them, Repent, and be baptized every one of you in the name of Jesus Christ for the remission of sins, and ye shall receive the gift of the Holy Ghost. For the promise is unto you, and to your children, and to all that are afar off, even as many as the Lord our God shall call.* (Acts 2:38–39)

It is evident here that the promise is the promise of the gift of the baptism with the Holy Spirit. It is settled then by both laws that the promise of Acts 2:39 is that of the gift of the Holy Spirit or baptism with the Holy Spirit. Let us then read the verse in that way, substituting this synonymous expression for the expression "the promise," "For the baptism with the Spirit is unto you, and to your children, and to all that are afar off, even as many as the Lord our God shall call."

"It is unto you," said Peter, that is, to the crowd assembled before him. There is nothing in that for us. We were not there. That crowd was all Jews, and we are not Jews. But Peter did not stop there. He went further and said, "And to your children," that

is, to the next generation of Jews or all future gen-
erations of Jews. Still there is nothing in it for us, for
we are not Jews. But Peter did not stop even there.
He went further and said, "And to all them that are
afar off." That does take us in. We are the Gentiles
who were once "afar off" but now "made nigh by the
blood of Christ" (Eph. 2:13). Lest there be any mistake about it whatever, Peter added "even as many
as the Lord our God shall call." So, on the very day of
Pentecost, Peter declared that the baptism with the
Holy Spirit is for every child of God in every coming
age of the church's history.

Some years ago at a ministerial conference in
Chicago, a minister of the Gospel from the South-
west came to me after a lecture on the baptism
with the Holy Spirit and said, "The church to
which I belong teaches that the baptism with the
Holy Spirit was for the apostolic age alone."

"I do not care," I replied, "what the church to
which you belong teaches or what the church to
which I belong teaches. The only question with me
is, what does the Word of God teach?"

"That is right," he said.

I then handed him my Bible and asked him to
read Acts 2:39, and he read, "For to you is the
promise, and to your children, and to all that are
afar off, even as many as the Lord our God shall
call unto him" (RV).

"Has He called you?" I asked.

"Yes, He certainly has."

"Is the promise for you then?"

"Yes, it is." He took it, and the result was a
transformed ministry.

Some years ago at a students' conference, the gatherings were presided over by a prominent Episcopalian minister, a man greatly honored and loved. I spoke at this conference on the baptism with the Holy Spirit and dwelt upon the significance of Acts 2:39. That night as we sat together after the meetings were over, this servant of God said to me, "Mr. Torrey, I was greatly interested in what you had to say today on the baptism with the Holy Spirit. If your interpretation of Acts 2:39 is correct, you have your case, but I doubt your interpretation of Acts 2:39. Let us talk it over." We did talk it over. Several years later, in July, 1894, I was at the students' conference at Northfield. As I entered the back door of Stone Hall that day, this Episcopalian minister entered the front door. Seeing me, he hurried across the hall and held out his hand and said, "You were right about Acts 2:39 at Knoxville, and I believe I have a right to tell you something better yet—that I have been baptized with the Holy Spirit."

I am glad that I was right about Acts 2:39, not that it is of any importance that I should be right, but the truth thus established is of immeasurable importance. It is glorious to be able to go literally around the world and face audiences of believers all over the United States, in the Sandwich Islands, in Australia and Tasmania and New Zealand, in China and Japan and India, in England and Scotland, Ireland, Germany, France, and Switzerland and to be able to tell them (and to know that I have God's sure Word under my feet when I do tell them) "You may all be baptized with the Holy Spirit." But that unspeakably joyous and glorious thought has its solemn side. If we may be baptized with the Holy Spirit, then we must be. If we are baptized with the Holy Spirit, then souls will be saved through our instrumentality who will not be saved if we are not thus baptized. If then we are not willing to pay the price of this baptism and therefore are not thus baptized, we will be responsible before God for every soul that might have been saved who was not saved because we did not pay the price and therefore did not obtain the blessing.

I often tremble for myself and for my peers in the ministry and not only for my peers in the ministry but for my peers in all forms of Christian work, even the most humble and obscure. Why? Because we are preaching error? No, alas, there are many in these dark days who are doing that, and I do tremble for them, but that is not what I mean now. Do I mean that I tremble because we are not preaching the truth? It is quite possible not to preach error and yet not preach the truth; many a man has never preached a word of error in his life but still is not preaching the truth. I do tremble for them, but that is not what I mean now. I mean that I tremble for those of us who are preaching the truth, the very truth as it is in Jesus, the truth as it is recorded in the written Word of God, the truth in its simplicity, its purity, and its fullness, but who are preaching it in "enticing words of man's wisdom" and not "in demonstration of the Spirit and of power" (1 Cor. 2:4), preaching it in the energy of the flesh and not in the power of the Holy Spirit. There is nothing more death dealing than the Gospel without the Spirit's power. "The letter killeth, but the spirit giveth life" (2 Cor. 3:6). It is awfully solemn business preaching the Gospel either from the pulpit or in more quiet ways. It means death or life to those that hear, and whether it means death or life depends very largely on whether we preach it with or without the baptism with the Holy Spirit.

We need repeated refilling with the Holy Spirit.

Even after one has been baptized with the Holy Spirit, no matter how definite that baptism may be, he needs to be filled again and again with the Spirit. This is the clear teaching of the New Testament. We read in Acts 2:4, "They were all filled with the Holy Ghost, and began to speak with other tongues, as the Spirit gave them utterance." Now, one of those who was present on this occasion and who therefore was filled at this time with the Holy Spirit was Peter. Indeed, he stands forth most prominently in the chapter as a man baptized with the Holy Spirit. We read in Acts 4:8, "Then Peter, filled with the Holy Ghost, said unto them...." Here we read again that Peter was filled with the Holy Ghost. Further down we read that being assembled together and praying, "they were all filled with the Holy Ghost, and they spake the word of God with boldness" (Acts 4:31). We are expressly told in the context that two of those present were John and Peter. Here, then, was a third instance in which Peter was filled with the Holy Spirit.

It is not enough that one be filled with the Holy Spirit once. We need a new filling for each new emergency of Christian service. The failure to realize this need of constant refillings with the Holy Spirit has led to many a man, who at one time was greatly used of God, being utterly laid aside. There are many today who once knew what it was to work in the power of the Holy Spirit who have lost their unction and their power. I do not say that the Holy Spirit has left them—I do not believe He has—but the manifestation of His presence and power has gone.

One of the saddest sights among us today is that of the men and women who once toiled for the Master in the mighty power of the Holy Spirit who are now practically of no use, or even a hindrance to the work, because they are trying to go in the power of the blessing received a year or five years or twenty years ago. For each new service that is to be conducted, for each new soul that is to be dealt with, for each new work for Christ that is to be performed, for each new day and each new emergency of Christian life and service, we should seek and obtain a new filling with the Holy Spirit. We must not "neglect" the gift that is in us (1 Tim. 4:14) but on the contrary "stir into flame" this gift (2 Tim. 1:6 RV, margin). Repeated fillings with the Holy Spirit are necessary to continuance and increase of power.

The question may arise: Should we call these new fillings with the Holy Spirit "fresh baptisms" with the Holy Spirit? To this we would answer that the expression "baptism" is never used in the Scriptures of a second experience, and there is something of an initiatory character in the very thought of baptism. So, if one wishes to be precisely biblical, it would seem to be better not to use the term "baptism" of a second experience but to limit it to the first experience. On the other hand, "filled with the Holy Spirit" is used in Acts 2:4 to describe the experience promised in Acts 1:5 where the words used are "ye shall be baptized with the Holy Ghost." And it is evident from this and from other passages that the two expressions are to a large extent practically synonymous. However, if we confine the expression "baptism with the Holy Spirit" to our first experience, we will be more exactly biblical, and it would be well to speak of one baptism but many fillings.

However, I would much prefer that one should speak about new or fresh baptisms with the Holy Spirit, standing for the all-important truth that we need repeated fillings with the Holy Spirit, than that he should so insist on exact phraseology that he would lose sight of the truth that repeated fillings are needed. In other words, I would rather have the right experience by a wrong name than the wrong experience by the right name. This much is as clear as day: that we need to be filled again and again and again with the Holy Spirit. I am sometimes asked, "Have you received the second blessing?" Yes, and the third and the fourth and the fifth and hundreds beside, and I am looking for a new blessing today.

Chapter 23

Obtaining the Baptism with the Holy Spirit

We come now to the question of first practical importance, namely, what a person must do in order to be baptized with the Holy Spirit. This question is answered in the plainest and most positive way in the Bible. A plain path is laid down in the Bible consisting of a few simple steps that anyone can take, and it is absolutely certain that anyone who takes these steps will enter into the blessing. This is, of course, a very positive statement, and we would not dare be so positive if the Bible were not equally positive. But what right have we to be uncertain when the Word of God is positive? There are seven steps in this path.

ACCEPTING JESUS CHRIST AS OUR LORD AND SAVIOR

The first step is that we accept Jesus Christ as our Savior and Lord. We read in Acts 2:38 (RV), "Repent ye, and be baptized every one of you in the name of Jesus Christ unto the remission of your sins; and ye shall receive the gift of the Holy

Ghost." Is not this statement as positive as that which we made above? Peter says that if we do certain things, the result will be, "Ye shall receive the gift of the Holy Ghost." All seven steps are in this passage, but we will refer later to other passages as throwing light upon this.

The first two steps are in the word "repent." "Repent," said Peter. What does it mean to repent? The Greek word for repentance means "an after-thought" or "change of mind." To repent then means to change your mind. But change your mind about what? About three things: about God, about Jesus Christ, and about sin. What the change of mind is about in any given instance must be determined by the context. As determined by the context in the present case, the change of mind is primarily about Jesus Christ. Peter had just said,

Let all the house of Israel know assuredly, that God hath made that same Jesus, whom ye have crucified, both Lord and Christ. Now when they heard this, they were pricked in their heart, [as well they might be] and said unto Peter and to the rest of the apostles, Men and brethren, what shall we do?

(Acts 2:36–37)

Then it was that Peter said, "Repent ye," "Change your mind about Jesus, change your mind from that attitude of mind that rejected Him and crucified Him to that attitude of mind that accepts Him as Lord and King and Savior." This then is the first step towards receiving the baptism with the Holy Spirit. Receive Jesus as Savior and

Lord; first of all receive Him as your Savior. Have you done that?

What does it mean to receive Jesus as Savior? It means to accept Him as the One who bore our sins in our place on the cross (see 2 Corinthians 5:21; Galatians 3:13) and to trust God to forgive us because Jesus Christ died in our place. It means to rest all our hope of acceptance before God upon the finished work of Christ upon the cross of Calvary. There are many who profess to be Christians who have not done this.

When you go to many who call themselves Christians and ask them if they are saved, they reply, "Yes." Then, if you put to them the question: "Upon what are you resting as the ground of your salvation?" they will reply something like this: "I go to church, I say my prayers, I read my Bible, I have been baptized, I have united with the church, I partake of the Lord's supper, I attend prayer meetings, and I am trying to live as near right as I know how." If these things are what you are resting upon as the ground of your acceptance before God, then you are not saved, for all these things are your own works (all proper in their places but still your own works), and we are distinctly told in Romans 3:20 that "by the deeds of the law there shall no flesh be justified in his sight."

However, if you go to others and ask them if they are saved, they will reply "Yes." And then if you ask them upon what they are resting as the ground of their acceptance before God, they will reply something to this effect, "I am not resting upon anything I ever did, or upon anything I am ever going to do; I am resting upon what Jesus Christ did for me when He bore my sins in His own body on the cross. I am resting in His finished work of atonement." If this is what you are really resting upon; then you are saved, you have accepted Jesus Christ as your Savior and have taken the first step towards the baptism with the Holy Spirit.

The same thought is taught elsewhere in the Bible, for example in Galatians 3:2. Here Paul asks of the believers in Galatia, "Received ye the Spirit by the works of the law, or by the hearing of faith?" Just what did he mean? On one occasion when Paul was passing through Galatia, he was detained there by some physical infirmity. We are not told what it was, but at all events, he was not so ill that he could not preach to the Galatians the Gospel, or glad tidings, that Jesus Christ had redeemed them from the curse of the law by becoming a curse in their place by dying on the cross of Calvary. These Galatians believed this testimony. This was the hearing of faith, and God set the stamp of His endorsement upon their faith by giving them as a personal experience the Holy Spirit.

But after Paul had left Galatia, certain Judaizers came down from Jerusalem, men who were substituting the law of Moses for the Gospel, and taught them that it was not enough that they simply believe in Jesus Christ. In addition to this, the Judaizers taught that they must keep the law of Moses, especially the law of Moses regarding circumcision, and that without circumcision they could not be saved. In other words, they could not be saved by simple faith in Jesus. (Compare Acts

15:1.) These young converts in Galatia became all upset. They did not know whether they were saved or not. They did not know what they ought to do, and all was confusion. It was just as when modern Judaizers come around and get after young converts and tell them that in addition to believing in Jesus Christ, they must keep the Mosaic seventh day Sabbath or they cannot be saved. This is simply the old controversy breaking out at a new point.

When Paul heard what had happened in Galatia, he was very indignant and wrote the epistle to the Galatians simply for the purpose of exposing the utter error of these Judaizers. He showed them how Abraham himself was justified before he was circumcised by simply believing God (see Galatians 3:6) and how he was circumcised after he was justified as a seal of the faith which he already had while he was in uncircumcision. In addition to this proof of the error of the Judaizers, Paul appeals to their own personal experience. He asks them if they received the Holy Spirit, and they replied that they had. He then asks them how they received the Holy Spirit: by keeping the law of Moses or by the hearing of faith, the simple accepting of God's testimony about Jesus Christ that their sins were laid upon Him, and that they are thus justified and saved. The Galatians had had a very definite experience of receiving the Holy Spirit, and Paul appeals to it and recalls to their minds how it was by the simple hearing of faith that they had received the Holy Spirit.

The gift of the Holy Spirit is God's seal upon the simple acceptance of God's testimony about

Jesus Christ, that our sins were laid upon Him, while trusting God to forgive us and justify us. This, then, is the first step towards receiving the Holy Spirit. But we must not only receive Jesus as Savior, we must also receive Him as Lord. Of this we will speak further in connection with another passage in the fourth step.

RENUNCIATION OF SIN

The second step in the path that leads into the blessing of being baptized with the Holy Spirit is renunciation of sin. Repentance, as we have seen, is a change of mind about sin as well as a change of mind about Christ: a change of mind from that attitude of mind that loves sin and indulges sin to that attitude of mind that hates sin and renounces sin. This, then, is the second step—renunciation of sin. The Holy Spirit is a Holy Spirit, and we cannot have both Him and sin. We must make our choice between the Holy Spirit and unholy sin. We cannot have both. He that will not give up sin cannot have the Holy Spirit. It is not enough that we renounce one sin or two sins or three sins or many sins; we must renounce all sin. If we cling to one single known sin, it will shut us out of the blessing.

Here we find the cause of failure in many people who are praying for the baptism with the Holy Spirit, going to conventions and hearing about the baptism with the Holy Spirit, reading books about the baptism with the Holy Spirit, perhaps spending whole nights in prayer for the baptism with the Holy Spirit, and yet obtaining nothing. Why? Because there is some sin to which they are clinging. People often say to me or write to me, "I have been praying for the baptism with the Holy Spirit for a year (five years, ten years, one man said twenty years). Why do I not receive?" In many such cases, I feel led to reply, "It is sin, and if I could look down into your heart this moment as God looks into your heart, I could put my finger on the specific sin." It may be what you are pleased to call a small sin, but there are no small sins. There are sins that concern small things, but every sin is an act of rebellion against God. Therefore no sin is a small sin. A controversy with God about the smallest thing is sufficient to shut one out of the blessing.

Mr. Finney tells of a woman who was greatly in earnest about the baptism with the Holy Spirit. Every night after the meetings, she would go to her room and pray way into the night. Her friends were afraid she would go insane, but no blessing came. One night as she prayed, some little matter of head adornment, a matter that would probably not trouble many Christians today, but a matter of controversy between her and God, came up (as it had often come up before) as she knelt in prayer. She put her hand to her head and took the pins out of her hair and threw them across the room and said, "There go!" Instantly the Holy Ghost fell upon her. It was not so much the matter of head adornment as the matter of controversy with God that had kept her out of the blessing.

If there is anything that always comes up when you get nearest to God, that is the thing to deal with.

Some years ago at a convention in a southern state, the presiding officer, a minister in the Baptist church, called my attention to a man and said, "That man is 'the pope' of our denomination in ———; everything he says goes, but he is not at all with us in this matter, but I am glad to see him here." This minister kept attending the meetings. At the close of the last meeting where I had spoken upon the conditions of receiving the baptism with the Holy Spirit, I found this man awaiting me in the vestibule.

He said, "I did not stand up on your invitation today."

I replied, "I saw you did not."

"I thought you said," he continued, "that you only wanted those to stand who could say they had absolutely surrendered to God?"

"That is what I did say," I replied.

"Well, I could not say that."

"Then you did perfectly right not to stand. I did not want you to lie to God."

"Say," he continued, "you hit me pretty hard today. You said if there was anything that always comes up when you get nearest to God, that is the thing to deal with. Now, there is something that always comes up when I get nearest to God. I am not going to tell you what it is. I think you know."

"Yes," I replied. (I could smell it.)

"Well, I simply wanted to say this to you."

This was on Friday afternoon. I had occasion to go to another city, and returning through that city the following Tuesday morning, the minister who had presided at the meeting was at the station. "I wish you could have been in our Baptist ministers' meeting yesterday morning," he said. "That man I pointed out to you from the north part of the state was present. He got up in our meeting and said, 'Fellow Christians, we have been all wrong about this matter,' and then he told what he had done. He had settled his controversy with God, had given up the thing which had always come up when he got nearest to God. Then he continued and said, 'Fellow Christians, I have received a more definite experience than I had when I was converted.'"

Just such an experience is awaiting many others, both minister and layman, just as soon as he will judge his sin, just as soon as he will put away the thing that is a matter of controversy between him and God, no matter how small the thing may seem. If anyone sincerely desires the baptism with the Holy Spirit, he should go alone with God and ask God to search him and bring to light anything in his heart or life that is displeasing to Him, and when He brings it to light, he should put it away. If after sincerely waiting on God, nothing is brought to light, then we may proceed to take the other steps. But there is no use praying, no use going to conventions, no use in reading books about the baptism with the Holy Spirit, no use in doing anything else, until we judge our sins.

AN OPEN CONFESSION OF OUR RENUNCIATION OF SIN AND OUR ACCEPTANCE OF JESUS CHRIST

The third step is an open confession of our renunciation of sin and our acceptance of Jesus Christ. After telling his hearers to repent in Acts

2:38, Peter continues and tells them to be "baptized every one of you in the name of Jesus Christ for the remission of sins." Heart repentance alone was not enough. There must be an open confession of that repentance, and God's appointed way of confession of repentance is baptism. None of those to whom Peter spoke had ever been baptized, and, of course, what Peter meant in that case was water baptism. But suppose one has already been baptized, what then? Even in that case there must be that for which baptism stands, namely, an open confession of our renunciation of sin and our acceptance of Jesus Christ. The baptism with the Spirit is not for the secret disciple but for the openly confessed disciple.

Undoubtedly, there are many today who are trying to be Christians in their hearts, many who really believe that they have accepted Jesus as their Savior and their Lord and have renounced sin, but they are not willing to make an open confession of their renunciation of sin and their acceptance of Christ. Such a person cannot have the baptism with the Holy Spirit. Someone may ask, "Do not the Friends (Quakers), who do not believe in water baptism, give evidence of being baptized with the Holy Spirit?" Undoubtedly, many of them do, but this does not alter the teaching of God's Word. God doubtless condescends in many instances where people are misled as to the teaching of His Word by their ignorance, if they are sincere, but that fact does not alter His Word. Even with a member of the congregation of Friends, who sincerely does not believe in water baptism, there must be that for which baptism stands before the blessing is received, namely, the open confession of acceptance of Christ and of renunciation of sin.

ABSOLUTE SURRENDER TO GOD

The fourth step is absolute surrender to God. This comes out in what has already been said, namely, that we must accept Jesus as Lord as well as Savior. It is stated explicitly in Acts 5:32: "And we are his witnesses of these things; and so is also the Holy Ghost, whom God hath given to them that obey him." That is the fourth step: "obey him," obedience.

But what does obedience mean? Someone will say, doing as we are told. Right, but doing how much that we are told? Not merely one thing or two things or three things or four things, but obedience is doing all things. The heart of obedience is in the will; the essence of obedience is the surrender of the will to God. It is going to God our heavenly Father and saying, "Heavenly Father, here I am. I am your property. You have bought me with a price. I acknowledge your ownership and surrender myself and all that I am absolutely to you. Send me where you will; do with me what you will; use me as you will." This is in most instances the decisive step in receiving the baptism with the Holy Spirit.

In the Old Testament typology it was when the whole burnt offering was laid upon the altar, nothing kept back within or without the sacrificial animal, that the fire came forth from the Holy Place where God dwelt and accepted and consumed the gift upon the altar. So it is today, in the fulfillment of the type, when we lay ourselves, a whole burnt offering, upon the altar, keeping nothing within or without back, that the fire of God, the Holy Spirit, descends from the real Holy Place, heaven (of which the Most Holy Place in the tabernacle was simply a type), and accepts the gift upon the altar. When we can truly say, "My all is on the altar," then we will not have long to wait for the fire. The lack of this absolute surrender is shutting many out of the blessing today. People turn the keys of almost every closet in their heart over to God, but there is some small closet of which they wish to keep the key themselves. Then the blessing does not come.

At a convention in Washington, D.C., on the last night, I had spoken on how to receive the baptism with the Holy Spirit. The Spirit Himself was present in mighty power that night. The chaplain of one of the houses had said to me at the close of the meeting, "It almost seemed as if I could see the Holy Spirit in this place tonight."

There were many to be dealt with. About two hours after the meeting closed (about eleven o'clock) a worker came to me and said, "Do you see that young woman over to the right with whom Miss W—— is speaking?"

"Yes."

"Well, she has been dealing with her for two hours, and she is in awful agony. Won't you come and see if you can help?"

I went into the seat behind this woman in distress and asked her her trouble. "Oh," she said, "I came from Baltimore to receive the baptism with the Holy Spirit, and I cannot go back to Baltimore until I have received Him."

"Is your will laid down?" I asked.

"I am afraid not."

"Will you lay it down now?"

"I cannot."

"Are you willing that God should lay it down for you?"

"Yes."

"Ask Him to do it."

She bowed her head in prayer and asked God to empty her of her will, to lay it down for her, to bring it into conformity to His will, in absolute surrender to His own. When the prayer was finished, I said, "Is it laid down?"

She said, "It must be. I have asked something according to His will. Yes, it is done."

I said, "Ask Him for the baptism with the Holy Spirit."

She bowed her head again in brief prayer and asked God to baptize her with the Holy Spirit and in a few moments looked up with peace in her heart and in her face. Why? Because she had surrendered her will. She had met the conditions, and God had given the blessing.

AN INTENSE DESIRE FOR THE BAPTISM WITH THE HOLY SPIRIT

The fifth step is an intense desire for the baptism with the Holy Spirit. Jesus says in John 7:37–39:

> *If any man thirst, let him come unto me, and drink. He that believeth on me, as the scripture hath said, out of his belly shall flow*

rivers of living water. But this spake he of the Spirit, which they that believe on him should receive.

Here again we have belief in Jesus as the condition of receiving the Holy Spirit, but we also have this, "If any man thirst." Doubtless, when Jesus spoke these words, He had in mind the Old Testament promise in Isaiah 44:3: "For I will pour water upon him that is thirsty, and floods upon the dry ground: I will pour my spirit upon thy seed, and my blessing upon thine offspring." In both of these passages thirst is the condition of receiving the Holy Spirit. What does it mean to thirst? When a man really thirsts, it seems as if every pore in his body has just one cry: "Water! Water! Water!" Apply this to the matter in question; when a man thirsts spiritually, his whole being has but one cry: "The Holy Spirit! The Holy Spirit! The Holy Spirit!"

As long as one fancies he can get along somehow without the baptism with the Holy Spirit, he is not going to receive that baptism. As long as one is casting about for some new kind of church, machinery, new style of preaching, or anything else by which he hopes to accomplish what the Holy Spirit only can accomplish, he will not receive the baptism with the Holy Spirit. As long as one tries to find some subtle system of interpretation to read out of the New Testament what God has put into it—namely, the absolute necessity that each believer receive the baptism with the Holy Spirit as a definite experience—he is not going to receive the baptism with the Holy Spirit. As long as a man tries to persuade himself that he has received the baptism with the Holy Spirit when he really has not, he is not going to receive the baptism with the Holy Spirit. But when one gets to the place where he sees the absolute necessity that he needs to be baptized with the Holy Spirit as a definite experience and desires this blessing at any cost, he is far on the way towards receiving it.

At a state YMCA Convention, where I had spoken on the baptism with the Holy Spirit, two ministers went out of the meeting side by side. One said to the other, "That kind of teaching leads either to fanaticism or despair." He did not attempt to show that it was unscriptural. He felt condemned and was not willing to admit his deficiency and seek to have it supplied. So, he tried to avoid the condemnation that came from the Word by this bright remark: "That kind of teaching leads either to fanaticism or despair." Such a man will not receive the baptism with the Holy Spirit until he is brought to himself and acknowledges honestly his need and intensely desires to have it supplied.

How different was another minister of the same denomination who came to me one Sunday morning at Northfield. I was to speak that morning on how to receive the baptism with the Holy Spirit. He said to me, "I have come to Northfield from ——— for just one purpose, to receive the baptism with the Holy Spirit, and I would rather die than go back to my church without receiving it."

I said, "My brother, you are going to receive it."

The following morning he came very early to my house. He said, "I have to go away on the early train, but I came around to tell you before I went that I have received the baptism with the Holy Spirit."

DEFINITE PRAYER FOR THE BAPTISM WITH THE HOLY SPIRIT

The sixth step is definite prayer for the baptism with the Holy Spirit. Jesus says in Luke 11:13, "If ye then, being evil, know how to give good gifts unto your children: how much more shall your heavenly Father give the Holy Spirit to them that ask him?" This is very explicit. Jesus teaches us that the Holy Spirit is given in answer to definite prayer—just ask Him. There are many who tell us that we should not pray for the Holy Spirit, and they reason it out very inaccurately. They say that the Holy Spirit was given as an abiding gift to the church at Pentecost, and why pray for what is already given? To this the late Rev. Dr. A. J. Gordon well replied that Jesus Christ was given as an abiding gift to the world at Calvary (see John 3:16), but what was given to the world as a whole, each individual in the world must appropriate for himself. Just so, the Holy Spirit was given to the church as an abiding gift at Pentecost, but what was given to the church as a whole, each individual in the church must appropriate for himself. God's way of appropriation is prayer.

Those who say we should not pray for the Holy Spirit go further still than this. They tell us that every believer already has the Holy Spirit (which we have already seen is true in a sense), and why pray for what we already have? To this the very simple answer is that it is one thing to have the Holy Spirit dwelling way back of consciousness in some hidden sanctuary of the being and something quite different, and vastly more, to have Him take possession of the whole house that He inhabits. But against all these inaccurate arguments we place the simple word of Jesus Christ: "How much more shall your heavenly Father give the Holy Spirit to them that ask him?" (Luke 11:13).

It will not do to say, as has been said, that this promise was for the time of the earthly life of our Lord, and to go back to the promise of Luke 11:13 is to forget Pentecost and to ignore the truth that now every believer has the indwelling Spirit. We find that after Pentecost as well as before, the Holy Spirit was given to believers in answer to definite prayer. For example, we read in Acts 4:31, "When they had prayed, the place was shaken where they were assembled together; and they were all filled with the Holy Ghost, and they spake the word of God with boldness." Again in Acts 8:15–16, we read that when Peter and John had come down and saw the believers in Samaria, they "prayed for them, that they might receive the Holy Ghost: (For as yet he was fallen upon none of them: only they were baptized in the name of the Lord Jesus.)" Again, in the epistle of Paul to the

Ephesians, Paul tells the believers in Ephesus that he was praying for them that they might be strengthened with power through His Spirit. (See Ephesians 3:16.) So right through the New Testament after Pentecost, as well as before, by specific teaching and illustrative example, we are taught that the Holy Spirit is given in answer to definite prayer.

At a Christian workers' convention in Boston, a believer came to me and said, "I notice that you are on the program to speak on the baptism with the Holy Spirit."

"Yes."

"I think that is the most important subject on the program. Now be sure and tell them not to pray for the Holy Spirit."

I replied, "My friend, I will be sure and not tell them that: for Jesus says, 'How much more shall your heavenly Father give the Holy Spirit to them that ask him?'"

"Yes, but that was before Pentecost."

"How about Acts 4:31; was that before Pentecost or after?"

He said, "It was certainly after."

"Well," I said, "take it and read it."

"'And when they had prayed, the place was shaken where they were assembled together; and they were all filled with the Holy Ghost, and they spake the word of God with boldness.'"

"How about Acts 8:15–16, was that before Pentecost or after?"

"Certainly, it was after."

"Take it and read it."

"'Who, when they were come down, prayed for them, that they might receive the Holy Ghost: For as yet he was fallen on none of them: only they were baptized in the name of the Lord Jesus.'"

He had nothing more to say. What was there more to say? But with me, it is not a matter of mere interpretation that the Holy Spirit is given in answer to definite prayer. It is a matter of personal and certain experience. I know just as well that God gives the Holy Spirit in answer to prayer as I know that water quenches thirst and food satisfies hunger. My first experience of being baptized with the Holy Spirit was while I waited upon God in prayer. Since then, time and again as I have waited on God in prayer, I have been definitely filled with the Holy Spirit. Often as I have knelt in prayer with others, as we prayed, the Holy Spirit has fallen upon us just as perceptibly as the rain ever fell upon and fructified the earth.

I shall never forget one experience in our church in Chicago. We were holding a noon prayer meeting of the ministers at the YMCA auditorium, in preparation of an expected visit to Chicago by Mr. Moody. At one of these meetings, a minister sprang to his feet and said, "What we need in Chicago is an all-night meeting of the ministers."

"Very well," I said. "If you will come up to Chicago Avenue Church Friday night at ten o'clock, we will have a prayer meeting, and if God keeps us all night, we will stay all night."

At ten o'clock on Friday night four or five hundred people gathered in the lecture rooms of the Chicago Avenue Church. They were not all ministers. They were not all men. Satan made a mighty attempt to ruin the meeting. First of all, three men got down by the door and knelt down by chairs and pounded and shouted until some of our heads seemed almost splitting. Some felt they must retire from the meeting, and when a brother went to expostulate with them and urge them that things be done decently and in order, they swore at the brother who made the protest. Still later, a man sprang up in the middle of the room and announced that he was Elijah. The poor man was insane. These things were distracting, and there was more or less of confusion until nearly midnight. Some thought they would go home. But it is a poor meeting that the devil can spoil, and some of us were there for a blessing and were determined to remain until we received it. About midnight God gave us complete victory over all the discordant elements. Then for two hours there was such praying as I have rarely heard in my life.

A little after two o'clock in the morning a sudden hush fell upon the whole gathering; we were all on our knees at the time. No one could speak; no one could pray; no one could sing; all you could hear was the subdued sobbing of joy, unspeakable and full of glory. The very air seemed trembling with the presence of the Spirit of God. It was now Saturday morning. The following morning, one of my deacons came to me and said, with bated breath, "I shall never forget yesterday morning until the last day of my life." But it was not by any means all emotion. There was solid reality that could be tested by practical tests.

A man went out of that meeting in the early morning hours and took a train for Missouri. When he had transacted his business in the town that he visited, he asked the proprietor of the hotel if there was any meeting going on in the town at the time. The proprietor said, "Yes, there is a protracted meeting going on at the Cumberland Presbyterian Church." The man was himself a Cumberland Presbyterian. He went to the church, and when the meeting was opened, he arose in his place and asked the minister if he could speak. Permission was granted, and with the power of the Holy Spirit upon him, he so spoke that fifty-eight or fifty-nine people professed to accept Christ on the spot.

A young man went out of the meeting in the early morning hours and took a train for a city in Wisconsin, and I soon received word from that city that thirty-eight young men and boys had been converted while he spoke. Another young man, one of our students in the Institute, went to another part of Wisconsin, and soon I began to receive letters from ministers in that neighborhood inquiring about him and telling how he had gone into the schoolhouses and churches and soldiers' home and how there were conversions wherever he spoke.

In the days that followed, men and women from that meeting went out over the earth, and I doubt if there was any country that I visited in my tour around the world, Japan, China, Australia, New Zealand, India, etc., in which I did not find someone who had gone out from that meeting with the power of God upon them. For me to doubt that

God fills men with the Holy Spirit in answer to prayer would be thoroughly unscientific and irrational. I know He does. And in a matter like this, I would rather have one ounce of believing experience than ten tons of unbelieving interpretation.

FAITH

The seventh and last step is faith. We read in Mark 11:24, "Therefore I say unto you, What things soever ye desire, when ye pray, believe that ye receive them, and ye shall have them." No matter how definite God's promises are, we only realize these promises experientially when we believe. For example, we read in James 1:5, "If any of you lack wisdom, let him ask of God, that giveth to all men liberally, and upbraideth not; and it shall be given him." Now that promise is as positive as a promise can be, but we read in the following verses:

But let him ask in faith, nothing wavering. For he that wavereth is like a wave of the sea driven with the wind and tossed. For let not that man think that he shall receive any thing of the Lord. A double minded man is unstable in all his ways.   (James 1:6–8)

The baptism with the Spirit, as we have already seen, is for those believers in Christ who have put away all sin and surrendered absolutely to God and who ask for it. But, even though we ask, there will be no receiving if we do not believe. There are many who have met the other conditions of receiving the baptism with the Holy Spirit and yet do not receive simply because they do not believe. They do not expect to receive, and they do not receive.

But there is a faith that goes beyond expectation, a faith that puts out its hand and takes what it asks on the spot. This comes out in the Revised Version of Mark 11:24: "Therefore I say unto you, All things whatsoever ye pray and ask for, believe that ye have received them, and ye shall have them." When we pray for the baptism with the Holy Spirit, we should believe that we have received (that is, that God has granted our prayer, and therefore it is ours), and then we will have the actual experience of that which we have asked.

When the Revised Version came out, I was greatly puzzled about the rendering of Mark 11:24. I had begun at the beginning of the New Testament and gone right through comparing the KJV with the Revised and comparing both with the best Greek text, but when I reached this passage, I was greatly puzzled. I read the KJV: "What things soever ye desire, when ye pray, believe that ye receive them, and ye shall have them," and that seemed plain enough. Then I turned to the Revised Version and read, "All things whatsoever ye pray and ask for, believe that ye have received them, and ye shall have them." I said to myself, "What a confusion of the tenses. Believe that ye have already received (past), and ye shall have afterwards (future). What nonsense."

Then I turned to my Greek Testament and found, whether sense or nonsense, the Revised

Version was the correct rendering of the Greek, but what it meant I did not know for years. Then one time I was studying and expounding to my church the First Epistle of John. I came to 1 John 5:14–15 (RV), and I read,

> *And this is the boldness which we have toward him, that, if we ask anything according to his will, he heareth us: and if we know that he heareth us whatsoever we ask, we know that we have the petitions which we have asked of him.*

Then I understood Mark 11:24. Do you see it? If not, let me explain it a little further. When we come to God in prayer, the first question to ask is, Is that which I have asked of God according to His will? If it is promised in His Word, of course, we know it is according to His will. Then we can say with 1 John 5:14: I have asked something according to His will, and I know He hears me. Then we can go further and say with the fifteenth verse: Because I know He hears what I ask, I know I have the petition which I asked of Him. I may not have it in actual possession, but I know it is mine because I have asked something according to His will and He has heard me and granted that which I have asked. What I thus believe, that I have received because the Word of God says so, I will afterwards have in actual experience.

Now apply this to the matter before us. When I ask for the baptism with the Holy Spirit, I have asked something according to His will, for Luke 11:13 and Acts 2:39 say so; therefore, I know my prayer is heard. Still further, I know because the prayer is heard that I have the petition which I have asked of Him; in other words, I know I have the baptism with the Holy Spirit. I may not feel it yet, but I have received. What I thus count mine resting upon the naked word of God, I will afterwards have in actual experience.

Some years ago I went to the students' conference at Lake Geneva, Wisconsin, with Mr. F. B. Meyer of London. Mr. Meyer spoke that night on the baptism with the Holy Spirit. At the conclusion of his address, he said, "If any of you wish to speak with Mr. Torrey or myself after the meeting is over, we will stay and speak with you." A young man came to me who had just graduated from one of the Illinois colleges. He said, "I heard of this blessing thirty days ago and have been praying for it ever since but do not receive. What is the trouble?"

"Is your will laid down?" I asked.

"No," he said, "I am afraid it is not."

"Then," I said, "there is no use praying until your will is laid down. Will you lay down your will?"

He said, "I cannot."

"Are you willing that God should lay it down for you?"

"I am."

"Let us kneel and ask Him to do it."

We knelt side by side, and I placed my Bible open at 1 John 5:14–15 (RV) on the chair before him. He asked God to lay down his will for him and empty him of his self-will and to bring his will into conformity with the will of God. When he had finished the prayer, I said, "Is it done?"

He said, "It must be. I have asked something according to His will, and I know He hears me, and I know I have the petition I have asked. Yes, my will is laid down."

"What is it you desire?"

"The baptism with the Holy Spirit."

"Ask for it."

Looking up to God he said, "Heavenly Father, baptize me with the Holy Spirit now."

"Did you get what you asked?" I asked.

"I don't feel it," he replied.

"That is not what I asked you," I said. "Read the verse before you," and he read, "'This is the boldness which we have toward him, that, if we ask anything according to his will, he heareth us.'"

"What do you know?" I asked.

He said, "I know if I ask anything according to His will He hears me."

"What did you ask?"

"I asked for the baptism with the Holy Spirit."

"Is that according to His will?"

"Yes, Acts 2:39 says so."

"What do you know then?"

"I know He has heard me."

"Read on."

"'And if we know that if he heareth us whatsoever we ask, we know that we have the petitions which we have asked of him.'"

"What do you know?" I asked.

"I know I have the petition I asked of Him."

"What was the petition you asked of Him?"

"The baptism with the Holy Spirit."

"What do you know?"

"I know I have the baptism with the Holy Spirit. I don't feel it, but God says so."

We arose from our knees and after a short conversation separated. I left Lake Geneva the next morning but returned in a few days. I met the young man and asked if he had really received the baptism with the Holy Spirit. He did not need to answer. His face told the story, but he did answer. He went into a theological seminary the following autumn, was given a church his junior year in the seminary, and had conversions from the outset. The next year on the Day of Prayer for Colleges, largely through his influence, there came a mighty outpouring of the Spirit upon the seminary. The president of the seminary wrote to a denominational paper that it was a veritable Pentecost, and it all came through this young man who received the baptism with the Holy Spirit through simple faith in the Word of God.

Anyone who will accept Jesus as his Savior and his Lord, put away all sin out of his life, publicly confess his renunciation of sin and acceptance of Jesus Christ, surrender absolutely to God, ask God for the baptism with the Holy Spirit, and take it by simple faith in the naked Word of God, can receive the baptism with the Holy Spirit right now. There are some who so emphasize the matter of absolute surrender that they ignore, or even deny, the necessity of prayer. It is always unfortunate when one so emphasizes one side of truth that he loses sight of another side which may be equally important. In this way, many lose the blessing which God has provided for them.

The seven steps given above lead with absolute certainty into the blessing. However, several questions arise.

Must we not wait until we know we have received the baptism with the Holy Spirit before we take up Christian work?

Yes, but how will we know? There are two ways of knowing anything in the Christian life. First, by the Word of God; second, by experience or feeling. God's order is to know things first of all by the Word of God. How one may know by the Word of God that he has received the baptism with the Holy Spirit has just been told. We have a right when we have met the conditions and have definitely asked for the baptism with the Holy Spirit to say, "It is mine," and to get up and go on in our work leaving the matter of experience to God's time and place. We get assurance that we have received the baptism with the Holy Spirit in precisely the same way that we get assurance of our salvation.

When an inquirer comes to you, whom you have reason to believe really has received Jesus but who lacks assurance, what do you do with him? Do you tell him to kneel down and pray until he gets assurance? Not if you know how to deal with a soul. You know that true assurance comes through the Word of God, that it is through what is "written" that we are to know that we have eternal life. (See 1 John 5:13.) So you take the inquirer to the written Word. For example, you take him to John 3:36. You tell him to read it.

He reads, "He that believeth on the Son hath everlasting life."

You ask him, "Who has everlasting life?"

He replies from the passage before him, "He that believeth on the Son."

"How many who believe on the Son have everlasting life?"

"Everyone that believes on the Son."

"Do you know this to be true?"

"Yes."

"Why?"

"Because God says so."

"What does God say?"

"God says, 'He that believeth on the Son hath everlasting life.'"

"Do you believe on the Son?"

"Yes."

"What have you then?"

He ought to say, "Everlasting life," but quite likely he will not. He may say, "I wish I had everlasting life." You point him again to the verse and by questions bring out what it says, and you hold him to it until he sees that he has everlasting life, sees that he has everlasting life simply because God says so. After he has assurance on the ground of the Word, he will have assurance by personal experience, by the testimony of the Spirit in his heart.

Now you should deal with yourself in precisely the same way about the baptism with the Holy

Spirit. Hold yourself to the word found in 1 John 5:14–15 and know that you have the baptism with the Spirit simply because God says so in His Word, whether you feel it or not. Afterwards, you will know it by experience.

God's order is always: first, His Word; second, belief in His Word; third, experience or feeling. We desire to change God's order and have first, His Word, then feeling, then we will believe, but God demands that we believe on His naked Word. "Abraham believed God, and it was accounted to him for righteousness" (Gal. 3:6; compare Genesis 15:6). Abraham had as yet no feeling in his body of new life and power. He just believed God, and feeling came afterwards. God demands of us today, as He did Abraham of old, that we simply take Him at His Word and count the thing ours which He has promised simply because He has promised it. Afterwards, we get the feeling and the realization of that which He has promised.

Will there be no manifestation of the baptism with the Spirit which we receive?

Will everything be just as it was before, and if it will, where is the reality and use of the baptism? Yes, there will be manifestation, very definite manifestation, but bear in mind what the character of the manifestation will be and when the manifestation is to be expected. When is the manifestation to be expected? After we believe, after we have received by simple faith in the naked Word of God.

And what will be the character of the manifestation? Here many go astray. They have read the wonderful experiences of Charles G. Finney, John Wesley, D. L. Moody, and others. These men tell us that when they were baptized with the Holy Spirit they had wonderful sensations. Finney, for example, describes it as great waves of electricity sweeping over him so that he was compelled to ask God to withhold His hand lest he die on the spot. Mr. Moody, on rare occasions, described a similar experience. That these men had such experiences, I do not for a moment question. The word of such men as Charles G. Finney, D. L. Moody, and others is to be believed, yet there is another reason why I cannot question the reality of these experiences. While these men doubtless had these experiences, there is not a passage in the Bible that describes such an experience. I am inclined to think the apostles had them, but if they had, they kept them to themselves. It is well that they did, for if they had put them on record, that is what we would be looking for today.

But what are the manifestations that actually occurred in the case of the apostles and the early disciples? New power in the Lord's work. We read at Pentecost that they were "all filled with the Holy Ghost, and began to speak with other tongues, as the Spirit gave them utterance" (Acts 2:4). Similar accounts are given of what occurred in the household of Cornelius and what occurred in Ephesus. All we read in the case of the apostle Paul is that Ananias came in and said, "Brother Saul, the Lord, even Jesus, that appeared unto thee in the way as thou camest, hath sent me, that thou mightest receive thy sight, and be filled with the Holy Ghost" (Acts 9:17). Then Ananias baptized him, and the next thing we read is that Paul went straight down to the synagogue and preached Christ so mightily in the power of the Spirit that he "confounded the Jews which dwelt at Damascus, proving that this is very Christ" (Acts 9:22).

So right through the New Testament, the manifestation that we are taught to expect, and the manifestation that actually occurred, was new power in Christian work, and that is the manifestation that we may expect today. We need not look too carefully for that. The thing for us to do is to claim God's promise and let God take care of the mode of manifestation.

May we not have to wait for the baptism with the Holy Spirit?

Did not the apostles have to wait ten days, and may we not have to wait ten days or even more? No, there is no necessity that we wait. We are told distinctly in the Bible why the apostles had to wait ten days. In Acts 2:1, we read, "And when the day of Pentecost was fully come" (literally "When the day of Pentecost was being fulfilled," RV, margin). Way back in the Old Testament, and back of that in the eternal counsels of God, the Day of Pentecost was set for the coming of the Holy Spirit and the gathering of the church, and the Holy Spirit could not be given until the Day of Pentecost was fully come. Therefore, the apostles had to wait until the Day of Pentecost was fulfilled, but there was no waiting after Pentecost.

There was no waiting, for example, in Acts 4:31. Scarcely had they finished the prayer when the place where they were gathered together was shaken, and "they were all filled with the Holy Ghost." There was no waiting in the household of Cornelius. They were listening to their first gospel sermon, and Peter said as the climax of his argument, "To him [that is Jesus] give all the prophets witness, that through his name whosoever believeth in him shall receive remission of sins" (Acts 10:43). No sooner had Peter spoken these words than they believed, and "the Holy Ghost fell on all them which heard the word" (Acts 10:44). There was no waiting in Samaria after Peter and John came down and told them about the baptism with the Holy Spirit and prayed with them. There was no waiting in Ephesus after Paul came and told them that there was not only the baptism of John unto repentance but the baptism of Jesus in the Holy Spirit. It is true that they had been waiting some time until then, but it was simply because they did not know that there was such a baptism for them.

Many may wait today because they do not know that there is the baptism with the Spirit for them, or they may have to wait because they are not resting in the finished work of Christ or because they have not put away sin or because they have not surrendered fully to God or because they will not definitely ask and believe and take. But the reason for the waiting is not in God; it is in ourselves. Anyone who will lay this book down at this point and take the steps which have been stated can immediately receive the baptism with the Holy Spirit.

I would not say a word to dissuade men from spending much time in waiting upon God in prayer for "they that wait upon the LORD shall renew their strength" (Isa. 40:31). There are few of us indeed in these days who spend as many hours as we should in waiting upon God. I can bear joyful testimony to the manifest outpourings of the Spirit that have come time and again as I have waited upon God through the hours of the night with fellow believers, but the point I would emphasize is that the baptism with the Holy Spirit may be had at once. The Bible proves this; experience proves it.

There are many waiting for feeling who ought to be claiming by faith. In these days we hear of many who say they are "waiting for their Pentecost." Some have been waiting weeks, some have been waiting months, some have been waiting years. This is not scriptural, and it is dishonoring to God. These Christians have an unscriptural view of what constitutes Pentecost. They have fixed it in their minds that certain manifestations are to occur. Since these particular manifestations, which they themselves have prescribed, do not come, they think they have not received the Holy Spirit. There are many who have been led into the error, already refuted in this book, that the baptism with the Holy Spirit always manifests itself in the gift of tongues. They have not received the gift of tongues; therefore, they conclude that they have not received the baptism with the Holy Spirit. But as already seen, one may receive the baptism with the Holy Spirit and not receive the gift of tongues. Others still are waiting for some ecstatic feeling. We do not need to wait at all. We may meet the conditions; we may claim the blessing at once on the ground of God's sure Word.

There was a time in my ministry when I was led to say that I would never enter my pulpit again until I had been definitely baptized with the Holy Spirit and knew it or until God in some way told me to go. I shut myself up in my study and day by day waited upon God for the baptism with the Holy Spirit. It was a time of struggle. The thought would arise, "Suppose you do not receive the baptism with the Holy Spirit before Sunday. How will it look for you to refuse to go into your pulpit." But, I held fast to my resolution. I had a more or less definite thought in my mind of what might happen when I was baptized with the Holy Spirit, but it did not come that way at all. One morning as I waited upon God, one of the quietest and calmest moments of my life, it was just as if God said to me, "The blessing is yours. Now go and preach."

If I had known my Bible then as I know it now, I might have heard that voice the very first day speaking to me through the Word. But I did not know it, and God in His infinite condescension, looking upon my weakness, spoke it directly to my heart. There was no particular ecstasy or emotion, simply the calm assurance that the blessing was mine. I went into my work, and God manifested His power in that work. Some time passed, I do not remember just how long, and I was sitting in that same study. I do not remember that I was thinking about this subject at all, but suddenly it was just as if I had been knocked out of my chair onto the floor. I lay upon my face crying, "Glory to God! Glory to God!" I could not stop. Some power, not my own, had taken possession of my lips and my whole person. I am not of an excitable, hysterical, or even emotional temperament, but I lost control of myself absolutely. I had never shouted before in my life, but I could not stop. When after a while I got control of myself, I went to my wife and told her what had happened. I tell this experience, not to magnify it, but to say that the time when this wonderful experience (which I cannot really fully describe) came was not the moment when I was baptized with the Holy Spirit. The moment when I was baptized with the Holy Spirit was in that calm hour when God said, "It is yours. Now go and preach."

There is an afternoon that I will never forget. It was July 8, 1894. It was at the Northfield Students' Convention. I had spoken that morning in the church on how to receive the baptism with the Holy Spirit. As I drew to a close, I took out my watch and noticed that it was exactly twelve o'clock. Mr. Moody had invited us to go up on the mountain that afternoon at three o'clock to wait upon God for the baptism with the Holy Spirit. As I looked at my watch, I said, "Gentlemen, it is exactly twelve o'clock. Mr. Moody has invited us to go up on the mountain at three o'clock to wait upon God for the baptism with the Holy Spirit. It is three hours until three o'clock. Some of you cannot wait three hours, nor do you need to wait. Go to your tent, go to your room in the hotel or in the buildings, go out into the woods, go anywhere where you can get alone with God, meet the conditions of the baptism with the Holy Spirit, and claim it at once."

At three o'clock we gathered in front of Mr. Moody's mother's house, four hundred fifty-six of us in all, all men from the eastern colleges. (I know the number because Mr. Paul Moody counted us as we passed through the gates down into the lots.) We commenced to climb the mountainside. After we had gone some distance, Mr. Moody said, "I do not think we need to go further. Let us stop here." We sat down, and Mr. Moody said, "Have any of you anything to say?" One after another, perhaps seventy-five men, arose and said words to this effect, "I could not wait until three o'clock. I have been alone with God, and I have received the baptism with the Holy Spirit." Then Mr. Moody said, "I can see no reason why we should not kneel right down here now and ask God that the Holy Spirit may fall on us as definitely as He fell on the apostles at Pentecost. Let us pray." We knelt down on the ground; some of us lay on our faces on the pine needles.

As we had gone up the mountainside, a cloud had been gathering over the mountain. As we began to pray, the cloud broke, and the raindrops began to come down upon us through the overhanging pine trees. However, another cloud, big with mercy, had been gathering over Northfield for ten days, and our prayers seemed to pierce that cloud allowing the Holy Ghost to fall upon us. It was a wonderful hour. There are many who will never forget it.

Anyone who reads this book may have a similar hour alone by himself now. He can take the seven steps one by one, and the Holy Spirit will fall upon him.

Chapter 24

The Work of the Holy Spirit in Prophets and Apostles

The work of the Holy Spirit in apostles and prophets is an entirely distinctive work. He imparts to apostles and prophets a special gift for a special purpose.

> *Now there are diversities of gifts, but the same Spirit...For to one is given by the Spirit the word of wisdom; to another the word of knowledge by the same Spirit; To another faith by the same Spirit; to another the gifts of healing by the same Spirit; To another the working of miracles; to another prophecy; to another discerning of spirits: to another divers kinds of tongues; to another the interpretation of tongues: But all these worketh that one and the selfsame Spirit, dividing to every man severally as he will...And God hath set some in the church, first apostles, secondarily prophets, thirdly teachers, after that miracles, then gifts of healing, helps, governments, diversities of tongues. Are all apostles? are all prophets?*

are all teachers? are all workers of miracles?
Have all the gifts of healing? do all speak
with tongues? do all interpret?
(1 Cor. 12:4, 8–11, 28–30)

It is evident from these verses that the work of the Holy Spirit in apostles and prophets is of a distinctive character.

The doctrine is becoming very common and very popular in our day that the work of the Holy Spirit in preachers and teachers and in ordinary believers, illuminating them and guiding them into the truth and opening their minds to understand the Word of God, is the same in kind and differs only in degree from the work of the Holy Spirit in prophets and apostles. It is evident from the passage just cited that this doctrine is thoroughly unscriptural and untrue. It overlooks the fact so clearly stated and carefully elucidated that while there is "the same Spirit" there are "diversities of gifts," "diversities of administrations," "diversities of operations" (1 Cor. 12:4–6), and that not all are prophets and not all are apostles. (See 1 Corinthians 12:29.)

A very scholarly and brilliant preacher seeking to minimize the difference between the work of the Holy Spirit in apostles and prophets and His work in other men calls attention to the fact that the Bible says of Bezaleel that God "filled him with the spirit of God" (Exod. 31:3) to devise the work of the tabernacle. (See Exodus 31:1–11.) The preacher gives this as a proof that the inspiration of the prophet does not differ from the inspiration of the artist or architect.

271

However, in doing this, he loses sight of the fact that the tabernacle was to be built after the "pattern of the tabernacle...which was showed thee [Moses] in the mount" (Exod. 25:9, 40), and that, therefore, it was itself a prophecy and an exposition of the truth of God. It was not mere architecture. It was the Word of God done into wood, gold, silver, brass, cloth, skin, etc. And Bezaleel needed as much special inspiration to reveal the truth in wood, gold, silver, brass, etc., as the apostle or prophet needs it to reveal the Word of God with pen and ink on parchment.

There is much reasoning in these days about inspiration that appears at first sight very learned but that will not bear much rigid scrutiny or candid comparison with the exact statements of the Word of God. There is nothing in the Bible more inspired than the tabernacle, and if the destructive critics would study it more, they would give up their ingenious but groundless theories as to the composite structure of the Pentateuch.

Truth hidden from man for ages and which they had not discovered and could not discover by the unaided processes of human reasoning has been revealed to apostles and prophets in the Spirit.

By revelation he had made known unto me the mystery; (as I wrote afore in few words, Whereby, when ye read, ye may understand my knowledge in the mystery of Christ) Which in other ages was not made known unto the sons of men, as it is now revealed

unto his holy apostles and prophets by the
Spirit. (Eph. 3:3–5)

The Bible contains truth that men had never discovered before the Bible stated it. It contains truth that men never could have discovered if left to themselves. Our heavenly Father, in great grace, has revealed this truth to us His children through His servants, the apostles, and the prophets. The Holy Spirit is the agent of this revelation.

There are many who tell us today that we should test the statements of Scripture by the conclusions of human reasoning or by the "Christian consciousness." The folly of all this is evident when we bear in mind that the revelation of God transcends human reasoning, and that any consciousness that is not the product of the study and absorption of Bible truth is not really a Christian consciousness.

We know the fact that the Bible does contain truth that man has never discovered not merely because it is so stated in the Scriptures, but we know it also as a matter of fact. There is not one of the most distinctive and precious doctrines taught in the Bible that men have ever discovered apart from the Bible. If our consciousness differs from the statements of this Book, which is so plainly God's Book, it is not yet fully Christian, and the thing to do is not to try to pull God's revelation down to the level of our consciousness but to tone our consciousness up to the level of God's Word.

The revelations made to the prophets were independent of their own thinking and were made to them by the Spirit of Christ which was in them.

These revelations were subjects of inquiry to their own minds as to their meaning. They were not their own thoughts but His.

> *Of which salvation the prophets have inquired and searched diligently, who prophesied of the grace that should come unto you: Searching what, or what manner of time the Spirit of Christ which was in them did signify, when it [He] testified beforehand the sufferings of Christ, and the glory that should follow. Unto whom it was revealed, that not unto themselves, but unto us they did minister the things, which are now reported unto you by them that have preached the gospel unto you with the Holy Ghost sent down from heaven; which things angels desire to look into.*
>
> *(1 Pet. 1:10–12)*

These words make it plain that a person in the prophets, and independent of the prophets, and that person, the Holy Spirit, revealed truth which was independent of their own thinking, which they did not altogether understand themselves, and regarding which it was necessary that they make diligent search and study. Another person than themselves was thinking and speaking, and they were seeking to comprehend what He said.

No prophet's utterance was of the prophet's own will, but he spoke from God, and the prophet was carried along in his utterance by the Holy Spirit.

We read in 2 Peter 1:21 (RV), "For no prophecy ever came by the will of man: but men spake from God, being moved by the Holy Ghost." Clearly then, the prophet was simply an instrument in the hands of another. As the Spirit of God carried him along, so he spoke.

It was the Holy Spirit who spoke in the prophetic utterances. It was His word that was upon the prophet's tongue.

We read in Hebrews 3:7, "Wherefore as the Holy Ghost saith, To day if ye will hear his voice." Further, we read,

> *Whereof the Holy Ghost also is a witness to us: for after that he had said before, This is the covenant that I will make with them after those days, saith the Lord, I will put my laws into their hearts, and in their minds will I write them.* *(Heb. 10:15–16)*

We read again in Acts 28:25, "And when they agreed not among themselves, they departed, after that Paul had spoken one word, Well spake the Holy Ghost by Esaias [Isaiah] the prophet unto our fathers." Still again we read in 2 Samuel 23:2, "The spirit of the LORD spake by me, and his word was in my tongue."

Over and over again in these passages, we are told that it was the Holy Spirit who was the speaker in the prophetic utterances and that it was His word, not theirs, that was upon the prophet's tongue. The prophet was simply the mouth by which the Holy Spirit spoke. As a man, that is, except as the Spirit taught him and used him, the prophet might be as fallible as other men are. However, when the Spirit was upon him and he was taken up and borne along by the Holy Spirit, he was infallible in his teachings, for his teachings in that case were not his own but the teachings of the Holy Spirit. When thus borne along by the Holy Spirit, it was God who was speaking and not the prophet.

For example, there can be little doubt that Paul had many mistaken notions about many things, but when he taught as an apostle in the Spirit's power, he was infallible. Rather, the Spirit who taught through him was infallible, and the consequent teaching was infallible, as infallible as God Himself. We do well, therefore, to carefully distinguish what Paul may have thought as a man and what he actually did teach as an apostle. In the Bible we have the record of what he taught as an apostle. There are those who think that Paul admits that he was not sure that he had the word of the Lord in 1 Corinthians 7:6, 25: "But I speak this by permission, and not of commandment...yet I give my judgment, as one that hath obtained mercy of the Lord." If this is the true interpretation of the passage (which is more than doubtful), we see how careful Paul was when he was not sure to note the fact, and this gives us additional certainty in all other passages.

It is sometimes said that Paul taught in his early ministry that the Lord would return during his lifetime and that in this he was, of course, mistaken. But Paul never taught anywhere that the Lord would return in his lifetime. It is true he says in 1 Thessalonians 4:17, "Then we which are alive and remain shall be caught up together with them in the clouds, to meet the Lord in the air: and so shall we ever be with the Lord." As he was still living when he wrote the words, he naturally and properly did not include himself with those who had already fallen asleep in speaking of the Lord's return. However, this is not to assert that he would remain alive until the Lord came. Quite probably at this period of his ministry, he entertained the hope that he might remain alive and consequently lived in an attitude of expectancy. But, the attitude of expectancy is the true attitude in all ages for each believer. It is quite probable that Paul expected that he would be alive at the coming of the Lord, but if he did so expect, he did not so teach. The Holy Spirit kept him from this as from all other errors in his teachings.

The Holy Spirit in the apostles taught not only the thoughts (or "concepts") but the words in which the thoughts were to be expressed.

We read in 1 Corinthians 2:13 (ASV), "Which things also we speak, not in words which man's wisdom teacheth, but which the Spirit teacheth; combining spiritual things with spiritual words." This passage clearly teaches that the words, as well as the thought, were chosen and taught by the Holy Spirit. This is also a necessary inference from the fact that thought is conveyed from mind to mind by words, and it is the words which express the thought. If the words were imperfect, the thought expressed in these words would necessarily be imperfect and to that extent be untrue. Nothing could be plainer than Paul's statement "in words...which the Spirit teacheth." The Holy Spirit has Himself anticipated all the modern ingenious and wholly unbiblical and false theories regarding His own work in the apostles.

The more carefully and minutely we study the wording of the statements of this wonderful Book, the more we will become convinced of the marvelous accuracy of the words used to express the thought. Very often the solution of an apparent difficulty is found in studying the exact words used. The accuracy, precision, and inerrancy of the exact words used is amazing. To the superficial student, the doctrine of verbal inspiration may appear questionable or even absurd. Any regenerated and Spirit-taught person who ponders the words of the Scripture day after day and year after year will become convinced that the wisdom of God is in the very words, as well as in the thought which the words endeavor to convey. A change of word or letter or tense or case or number in many instances would land us into contradiction or untruth, but when taking the words exactly as written, difficulties disappear and truth shines forth. The divine origin of nature shines forth more clearly in the use of a microscope as we see the perfection of form and

adaptation of means to an end of the minutest parti-
cles of matter. In a similar manner, the divine origin
of the Bible shines forth more clearly under the microscope as we notice the perfection with which the
turn of a word reveals the absolute thought of God.

Someone may ask, "If the Holy Spirit is the
author of the words of Scripture, how do we account
for variations in style and diction? How do we explain, for instance, that Paul always used Pauline
language and John Johannine language, etc.?" The
answer to this is very simple. If we could not account at all for this fact, it would have but little
weight against the explicit statement of God's Word
with anyone who is humble enough and wise
enough to recognize that there are a great many
things which he cannot account for at all which
could be easily accounted for if he knew more. However, these variations are easily accounted for. The
Holy Spirit is quite wise enough and has quite facil-
ity enough in the use of language in revealing truth
to and through any given individual to use words,
phrases, forms of expression, and idioms in that
person's vocabulary and forms of thought and to
make use of that person's peculiar individuality.
Indeed, it is a mark of the divine wisdom of this
Book that the same truth is expressed with absolute
accuracy in such widely variant forms of expression.

**The utterances of the apostles and the prophets were the
Word of God. When we read these words, we are listening
not to the voice of man, but to the voice of God.**

We read in Mark 7:13, "Making the word of
God of none effect through your tradition, which

ye have delivered: and many such like things do ye." Jesus had been setting up the law given through Moses against the Pharisaic traditions. In doing this, He expressly says in this passage that the law given through Moses was "the word of God." In 2 Samuel 23:2, we read, "The spirit of the LORD spake by me, and his word was in my tongue." Here again, we are told that the utterance of God's prophet was the word of God. In a similar way God says in 1 Thessalonians 2:13,

> For this cause also thank we God without ceasing, because, when ye received the word of God which ye heard of us, ye received it not as the word of men, but as it is in truth, the word of God, which effectually worketh also in you that believe.

Here Paul declares that the word which he spoke, taught by the Spirit of God, was the very word of God.

Chapter 25

The Work of the Holy Spirit in Jesus Christ

J esus Christ Himself is the one perfect manifestation in history of the complete work of the Holy Spirit in man.

Jesus Christ was begotten of the Holy Spirit.

> And the angel answered and said unto her,
> The Holy Ghost shall come upon thee, and
> the power of the Highest shall overshadow
> thee: therefore also that holy thing which
> shall be born of thee shall be called the Son
> of God.   (Luke 1:35)

As we have already seen, in regeneration the believer is begotten of God, but Jesus Christ was begotten of God in His original generation. He is the only begotten Son of God. (See John 3:16.) It was entirely by the Spirit's power working in Mary that the Son of God was formed within her. The regenerated man has a carnal nature received from his earthly father and a new nature imparted by God. Jesus Christ had only the one holy nature that which in man is called the new nature. Nevertheless, He was a real man as He had a human mother.

Jesus Christ led a holy and spotless life and offered Himself without spot to God through the working of the Holy Spirit.

We read in Hebrews 9:14, "How much more shall the blood of Christ, who through the eternal Spirit offered himself without spot to God, purge your conscience from dead works to serve the living God." Jesus Christ met and overcame temptations, as other men may meet and overcome them, in the power of the Holy Spirit. He was tempted and suffered through temptation (Heb. 2:18). He was tempted in all points like as we are (Heb. 4:15), but never once in any way did He yield to temptation. He was tempted entirely apart from sin (Heb. 4:15), but He won His victories in a way that is open for all of us to win victory in the power of the Holy Spirit.

Jesus Christ was anointed and fitted for service by the Holy Spirit.

We read in Acts 10:38, "How God anointed Jesus of Nazareth with the Holy Ghost and with power: who went about doing good, and healing all that were oppressed of the devil; for God was with him." In a prophetic vision of the coming Messiah in the Old Testament we read,

> *The spirit of the Lord GOD is upon me; because the LORD hath anointed me to preach*

good tidings unto the meek; he hath sent me
to bind up the brokenhearted, to proclaim
liberty to the captives, and the opening of the
prison to them that are bound.   (Isa. 61:1)

In Luke's record of the earthly life of our
Lord in Luke 4:14 we read, "And Jesus returned
in the power of the Spirit into Galilee: and there
went out a fame of him through all the region
round about." In a similar way, Jesus said of
Himself when speaking in the synagogue in Nazareth,

The Spirit of the Lord is upon me, because
he hath anointed me to preach the gospel to
the poor; he hath sent me to heal the broken-
hearted, to preach deliverance to the cap-
tives, and recovering of sight to the blind, to
set at liberty them that are bruised, To
preach the acceptable year of the Lord.
(Luke 4:18–19)

All these passages contain the one lesson that
it was by the special anointing with the Holy Spirit
that Jesus Christ was qualified for the service to
which God had called Him. As He stood in the Jordan after His baptism, "the Holy Ghost descended
in a bodily shape like a dove upon him" (Luke
3:22). It was then and there that He was anointed
with the Holy Spirit, baptized with the Holy Spirit,
and equipped for the service that lay before Him.
Jesus Christ received His equipment for service in
the same way that we receive ours—by a definite
baptism with the Holy Spirit.

Jesus Christ was led by the Holy Spirit in His movements here upon earth.

We read in Luke 4:1, "And Jesus being full of the Holy Ghost returned from Jordan, and was led by the Spirit into the wilderness." Living as a man here upon earth and setting an example for us, each step of His life was under the Holy Spirit's guidance.

Jesus Christ was taught by the Spirit who rested upon Him. The Spirit of God was the source of His wisdom in the days of His flesh.

In the Old Testament prophecy of the coming Messiah we read,

> *And the spirit of the LORD shall rest upon him, the spirit of wisdom and understanding, the spirit of counsel and might, the spirit of knowledge and of the fear of the LORD; And shall make him of quick understanding in the fear of the LORD: and he shall not judge after the sight of his eyes, neither reprove after the hearing of his ears.*
> *(Isa. 11:2–3)*

Further on in Isaiah 42:1 (RV), we read, "Behold my servant, whom I uphold; my chosen, in whom my soul delighteth: I have put my spirit upon him: he shall bring forth judgment to the Gentiles." Matthew tells us in Matthew 12:17–18 that this prophecy was fulfilled in Jesus of Nazareth.

The Holy Spirit abode upon Jesus in all His fullness, and the words He spoke, consequently, were the very words of God.

We read in John 3:34, "For he whom God hath sent speaketh the words of God: for God giveth not the Spirit by measure unto him."

After His resurrection, Jesus Christ gave commandments to His apostles whom He had chosen through the Holy Spirit.

We read in Acts 1:2, "Until the day in which he was taken up, after that he through the Holy Ghost had given commandments unto the apostles whom he had chosen." This relates to the time after His resurrection, and so we see Jesus still working in the power of the Holy Spirit even after His resurrection from the dead.

Jesus Christ wrought His miracles here on earth in the power of the Holy Spirit.

In Matthew 12:28, we read, "I cast out devils by the Spirit of God." It is through the Spirit that miracle working power was given to some in the church after our Lord's departure from this earth (see 1 Cor. 12:9–10), and in the power of the same Spirit, Jesus Christ wrought His miracles.

It was by the power of the Holy Spirit that Jesus Christ was raised from the dead.

We read in Romans 8:11, "But if the Spirit of him that raised up Jesus from the dead dwell in you, he that raised up Christ from the dead shall also quicken your mortal bodies by his Spirit that dwelleth in you." The same Spirit who is to quicken our mortal bodies and is to raise us up in some future day raised up Jesus.

The following things are plainly evident from this study of the work of the Holy Spirit in Jesus Christ.

First of all, we see the completeness of His humanity. He lived, He thought, He worked, He taught, and He conquered sin and won victories for God in the power of that very same Spirit whom it is our privilege also to have.

In the second place, we see our own utter dependence upon the Holy Spirit. If it was in the power of the Holy Spirit that Jesus Christ, the only begotten Son of God, lived and worked, achieved and triumphed, how much more dependent are we upon Him at every turn of life and in every phase of service and every experience of conflict with Satan and sin.

The third thing that is evident is the wondrous world of privilege, blessing, and victory and conquest that is open to us. The same Spirit by which Jesus was originally begotten is at our disposal for us to be begotten again of Him. The same Spirit by which Jesus offered Himself without spot to God is at our disposal that we also may offer ourselves without spot to Him. The same Spirit by which Jesus was anointed for service is at our disposal that we may be anointed for service. The same Spirit who led Jesus Christ in His movements here on earth is ready to lead us today. The same Spirit who taught Jesus and imparted to Him wisdom and understanding, counsel and might, and knowledge and the fear of the Lord is here to teach us.

Jesus Christ is our pattern: "He that saith he abideth in him ought himself also so to walk, even as he walked" (1 John 2:6), "the firstborn among many brethren" (Rom. 8:29). Whatever He realized through the Holy Spirit is for us also to realize today.